The Book of Job
A Short Reading

The Book of Job
A Short Reading

Roland E. Murphy, O. Carm.

PAULIST PRESS
New York / Mahwah, N.J.

The transliteration of Hebrew words is made in a simplified form for the sake of readers' pronunciation.

Cover illustration: William Blake (1757–1827), "Job's Sacrifice," illustration for the Book of Job, III, 45, pl. 18, watercolor. The Pierpont Morgan Library, New York, N.Y., USA. Courtesy The Pierpont Morgan Library/Art Resource, N.Y.

Cover design by Morris Berman Studio

Copyright © 1999 by Roland E. Murphy, O. Carm.

Library of Congress Cataloging-in-Publication Data

Murphy, Roland Edmund, 1917–
    The book of Job : a short reading / Roland E. Murphy.
        p.   cm.
    Includes bibliographical references and index.
    ISBN 0-8091-3889-1 (alk. paper)
    1. Bible. O.T. Job Commentaries. I. Title.
BS1415.3.M87   1999
223′.107—dc21   99-34535
                                                                         CIP

Published by Paulist Press
997 Macarthur Boulevard
Mahwah, New Jersey 07430

www.paulistpress.com

Printed and bound in the
United States of America

Contents

Gratefully dedicated to the Carmelites,
past and present, of Whitefriars Hall

Abbreviations

ANET   J. Pritchard (ed.), *Ancient Near Eastern Texts* (3rd ed. Princeton University Press, 1978)

NAB   New American Bible

NIV   New International Version

NRSV   New Revised Standard Version

NBE   Nueva Biblia Española

OTL   Old Testament Library

OTP   J. Charlesweorth (ed.), *The Old Testament Pseudepigrapha* (2 vols.; New York, 1983–85)

Vulg   Vulgate

Preface

THE TITLE OF THIS LITTLE BOOK is important: the aim is to offer a short, succinct commentary, and provide a specific reading. Short, because the writer is convinced that most people will not pick up a long commentary, no matter how excellent it be. Many find it a chore even to read the Book of Job from beginning to end. The reasons for this state of affairs are doubtless many, but it is a deplorable fact. A specific reading, because there are differing interpretations of this book, and here is one among many: but it is not the only possible one. Indeed, readers of these lines may have already formed an idea of what the book is about. In that case, they may find it challenging to consider other views. I aim to answer the second part of the clever title of an intriguing article by D. J. Clines. He asks, "Why is there a Book of Job, and what does it do to you if you read it?" (W. Beuken, ed. *The Book of Job* [BETL 114; Leuven: University Press, 1994] 1–20). Yes, what does reading the book do to you? Among other things, Clines claims (p. 20) that "by its charm and its force, by its rhetoric and its passion it persuades readers of ideas that cannot be defended...." The reader is invited to see if he or she agrees with that or any other conclusion. What does the book do to you if you read it?

The present writer has lectured on the Book of Job, and almost as many times he has wondered why so many students do not become intrigued by a work that is considered on all sides to be a masterpiece. There may be several reasons, such as the uncertainty in the text, which is reflected in varying translations, or the apparent repetition within the chapters that suggests mere sameness and begets boredom, or the wide variety of interpretations as to what the book is all about. The present reflections are intended to prompt a more intense but leisurely reading and thus to achieve greater understanding and love of the book. That comes at a price—the price, for example, of neglecting extensive discussion of many of the severe textual problems for which this book is notorious, such as 19:25–27, 36:16–20, or 42:1–6. However, there are many studies and commentaries that remedy this lacuna in part. It is irksome for readers to be dependent upon the accuracy of a translator, but such is the history of the transmission of the Bible.

This exposition aims at helping whoever utilizes the current English translations, such as the New American Bible, the New Revised Standard Version, the New International Version, the Jerusalem Bible, or the New Jewish Version (Tanakh), all of which have much in common. The device of a marginal indication of chapter and verse(s) will enable readers to concentrate on smaller units within the larger frame. They do not represent stanzas or strophic divisions within poems; they merely follow the train of thought. These comments have to be succinct, for the sake of concentrating upon what is generally agreed to be the meaning. At the same time, they can provoke the reader to a more aggressive analysis of the book. When Job is considered a defiant hero, the roles of the three friends, of Elihu, and even of the satan, may not be appreciated as they should be. Is there a dominant point of view, or many, or none, in the book? What is the specific purpose of the work? Is it a book of theodicy, exploring divine justice, or the suffering of the innocent? Or is it about how to speak about God in the midst of suffering? Read the text of the Book of Job carefully with the help of this commentary. *Tolle, lege.*

1

Introduction

AT THE OUTSET IT WOULD BE PRUDENT to consider the useful information that has emerged concerning the book in general, to lay out certain assumptions, and at the same time to suggest various strategies employed in reading the book.

1. *Do we know anything about the author(s)?* Nothing, not even if there were one or (as most think) many authors. Whatever the number, great poetry is the result. At no point in the book does the poetic quality of the work sag. Indeed, it would be extremely hypothetical, not to say unwise, to try to distinguish between various parts of the work on the basis of the poetry alone. The arguments for multiple authorship usually proceed on an interpretive basis. For example, many judge that the words of the unnamed speaker of the wisdom poem in 28:1–28 do not "fit" into the work, or that the speeches of Elihu (chaps. 32–37) seem to add nothing to the work and hence are from another hand. This kind of reasoning is hypothetical, tenuous, and ultimately counterproductive. Even if one could demonstrate that these chapters or any other portions were due to another hand, or even a later addition by the one author, we must try to understand *why* they were added. Whoever might have been the putative editor who added the material, the additions were doubtless intended to make sense. What the readers now have before them are 42 chapters handed down as a unit. Can these be explained without recourse to mere hypotheses concerning authors and additions? There is no denying the differences between the traditional

Hebrew text and the (shorter) ancient Greek version (the Septuagint). Indeed, the text of Job is often corrupt and the evidence of the Greek and other ancient translations is a help to improving our understanding of many passages. But all the ancient versions had the 42 chapters of the Hebrew text to deal with. There is a widely held view that the text has suffered some dislocation in chapters 26 through 27, where Zophar disappears and Job seems to utter words that conflict with his previous protests. But such a claim is debatable. However successful a restoration of the sequence of verses might seem to be, it remains hypothetical, and one is left with the task of making sense of the text as it stands. Every reader of Job soon becomes aware that at times the text presumed by an interpreter will differ. There is no escape from problematic texts.

2. *Did Job even exist?* It is wise to distinguish between two Jobs: an historical person and a literary character. Apart from the book itself, we learn of a Job who is mentioned along with Noah and Dan(i)el in Ezekiel 14:14, 20. All three were renowned for their righteousness, but even such holy men as these would not be enough to preserve Jerusalem from destruction, says the Lord (Ezek 14:12–20). Noah is known of course as the hero preserved from the devastation of the Flood, and Danel is perhaps a just judge known from the Aqhat legend discovered in the ancient Canaanite city of Ugarit (about 1500 B.C.). But it is Job that occupies our attention. At least by the time of Ezekiel (circa 600 B.C.) he was known as an extraordinarily righteous person. None of these three are Israelites, and the Book of Job identifies him as being from the land of Uz (probably somewhere in Edom, where his three friends also hail from), and thus a non-Israelite. The events of Job 1–2 are tailored to fit such a character as this Job, who came down in tradition as a holy man. On the basis of the mention in Ezekiel, one would hardly have reason to suppose that he was any more historical than Noah or Danel.

When we consider the second Job, the Job who is the hero of the book, the issue of his historical existence is not the question to raise. The prologue and ending of the book would suggest that we are dealing with a saintly character of legend. Even more striking is the nature of the dialogue in chapters 3 through 31, which strongly supports the idea that this "second" Job is primarily a literary character. No one sitting in pain on a refuse mound would be in a position to pronounce the powerful poetical periods we find on his lips (nor are the words of the three merely extemporaneous remarks!). Rather, the scenes in Job are a *literary* creation. We may leave aside the hypothesis of an oral transmission, since that would be irrelevant to our main point: the Book of Job is a product of great poetic art. It is simply too much a work of genius to be tossed off in several minutes of conversation. The whole work has been carefully thought out and powerfully expressed. Let one argument suffice for this claim: the exquisite use of irony throughout the book.

Adopting a commonly accepted understanding of irony, I understand it to mean that a statement can be seen, in the light of later developments, to have a second meaning that negates or modifies what it seems to say. Perhaps the supreme irony of the book is the final reversal: the proponents of orthodoxy and defenders of God are reprimanded and the rebellious Job is upheld by the Lord. In this light, many of the statements uttered by the friends or even by Job can be seen to be correct, but not in the sense they were intended. For example, in 9:17 Job says that God attacks him "without cause"—while unbeknownst to him God has admitted this, using that very phrase in speaking to the satan in 2:12. In 11:5, Zophar expresses the wish that God might reveal to Job the secrets of wisdom. In the end, his wish will be fulfilled differently than he intended. In a derisive putdown of Job in 12:3, Eliphaz asks whether Shaddai, the Almighty, gains anything by Job's righteousness. The prologue has forewarned the attentive reader that God does stand to gain if Job remains faithful (despite his bold language), thus defeating the satan's claim in 1:11; 2:5. In 22:27–30 Eliphaz assures Job that God will listen to his (Job's) prayers, and then in 42:9 God does accept Job's intercession, *but* on behalf of the three friends. In 8:20 Bildad confidently proclaims that God will not reject the blameless *(tam),* unaware of course that in the prologue (1:8) the Lord had boasted that Job was indeed blameless. These little ironies are not always apparent to one who does not read the book in Hebrew. A common objection raised concerning the debate is that Job and the three do not seem to conduct an orderly discussion. True, their repartee does not follow the rules of western logic; the ironies are strewn through the work, and they form a network of debate characteristic of the disputants.

3. *The date.* Any dating of the book has to proceed on the basis of tentative evidence, and nothing is certain. First of all, those who distinguish several authors propose several dates, suggesting that the legend of Job (prologue and epilogue) is the oldest part of the book, and thus certainly pre-exilic. A linguistic analysis of the work does not yield a sure date, and the result is the same if one attempts to assign a date on the basis of the theology. For example, it is argued that because it is concerned with the problem of suffering, such as Israel experienced in the exile,the book must have been written at the time of the exile (about 587 B.C.), but there is no cogency to such a claim. The issues of suffering and personal responsibility are in a sense timeless. We cannot ascertain with certainty the date (of even the final form) of the Book of Job. Perhaps the majority of scholars date it with most of the biblical wisdom literature in the postexilic period, but there is no hard data for this.

4. *Wisdom.* We have just indicated that Job is classified among the wisdom books. A relatively small minority would disagree, but have no positive proposal to suggest in its place. Reasons for classifying Job within Israelite wisdom literature are fairly straightforward. As usual, there is no mention of typical events from Israel's history, such as the patriarchal promises, Exodus, Sinai and covenant, and so forth. This negative sign is strengthened by several references to wisdom. First of all there is the wisdom poem in Job 28 (vv 12, 20, "Where is wisdom to be found?"). There are several references to "the wise": Eliphaz has recourse to their traditions (15:18); Elihu addresses himself to the "wise" in 34:2 (cf. 34:10, 34) and his objective is to teach Job "wisdom" (33:33). Job himself speaks sarcastically of the wisdom of the three friends (12:2; 13:5).

While the use of the word and its synonyms is important, even more telling is the approach to reality manifested in the book, such as the reflections about creation in 9:5–10; 12:7–15; 36:24–37:13; 38:1–39:30.

The problem of divine justice and retribution is an issue that receives particular emphasis in the wisdom tradition. Whereas the traditional theory is reflected in the Book of Proverbs, it is only in Job and Ecclesiastes that it is seriously controverted. The theory is pretty much a biblical mindset: there is a connection between sin and suffering—prosperity is attained by the wise and virtuous, but destruction is the fate of the foolish and wicked. The Book of Job is a vehement attack on this view. It does not square with reality, and specifically with Job's experience. Although the problem is raised in other books of the Bible (Gen 18:22–32; Jer 12:1–5; Pss 37 and 73), it is particularly the subject of debate from Proverbs all through sapiential literature down to the Wisdom of Solomon at the beginning of the Christian era. Thus it is a genuine wisdom problem. Proverbs and Sirach generally hold to the traditional view, while Job and Ecclesiastes argue against it. But it would be a mistake to regard these latter works as "anti-wisdom." Rather, they open wide the windows of wisdom and purify it by criticizing foolhardy conclusions.

5. *How does Job fit in with the ancient Near Eastern wisdom that has also been handed down?* It can be said at once that no true parallel to Job as yet has appeared. Works from Mesopotamia and Egypt have been compared, but there is no question of literary dependence on one or the other work. Rather, Job is used as the criterion insofar as some scholars speak of a "Sumerian" or "Babylonian" Job. But the comparison is shortsighted. Who is there in any age who has not suffered unjustly, at least in one's own judgment, and also questioned God? In the ancient world, the divinity or divinities were held responsible for human affliction, and thus they were sharply accused in various works. The pertinent texts from Mesopotamia and Egypt have been translated into modern European languages (for English, see J. Pritchard, *ANET*). The most

frequently mentioned counterpart to Job is the Babylonian "I Will Praise the Lord of Wisdom" (*ANET,* 434–37, dated between 1500 and 1200). Some of the most pertinent lines are: "Oh, that I only knew that these things are well pleasing to a god! What is good in one's sight is evil for a god. What is bad in one's own mind is good for his god. Who can understand the counsel of the gods in the midst of heaven?" Such lines reflect puzzlement over the ways of divinity in dealing with people. However, the poem is really a hymn in praise of Marduk, because he delivers the righteous sufferer. There is no dialogue, and the problem of unjust treatment is merely referred to; it is not the focus of the work, as is the case with Job. Another work, "The Babylonian Theodicy" (*ANET,* 439–440) is an acrostic poem in which a faithful servant of god, who is nevertheless suffering, has a dialogue with his friend. But the relationship is amicable and the repartee is mild. In the end there is an admission that the gods have made human beings evil (lines 276–80); in that case, one can no longer speak of a parallel with Job.

A third work, "The Dialogue of Pessimism" (*ANET,* 438), is related to Qoheleth (Ecclesiastes) rather than to Job. It is a dialogue, but not concerning the divine-human relationship. The Egyptian "Dispute over Suicide" or "Dispute between a man and his Ba" (*ANET,* 405–407) deals with a desire for death, and this is a prominent feature in Job (3:11–19; 10:21–22). But this topic is too general to suggest real similarity, much less dependence. In short, the extrabiblical literature of antiquity offers little evidence of direct influence on the biblical work. It is to be expected that people of all ages and cultures would complain of suffering, and blame the divinity. But no one has exploited this theme with the same intensity as the Book of Job. It is hardly enlightening to say that in the ancient literature of Israel's neighbors, literary expression was given to the problem of the suffering. The treatment in Job is so far superior that there is no sufficient reason for solid comparison. The most one can say is that there is a precedent for this kind of literature before Job was written—but it can be explained by the universal experience of inexplicable suffering.

2

The Prologue
1:1–2:13

1:1–5. The prologue has the coloring of a folk tale about a holy and prosperous patriarchal figure: Job has a large family, great possessions of sheep, camels, oxen and asses, and is tended by servants. The final tag is not an exaggeration: he is one of the richest men of the East (literally, "the sons of Kedem"). His extreme attention to the rights of God is portrayed by his providing burnt offerings for his children in expiation for any possible wrongdoing. They may have "blasphemed" in their hearts. Literally, the text reads "blessed" —a euphemism presumably employed in Jewish tradition for "curse" when the latter word is used with God as the object; cf. 1:11; 2:5,9. This is a key word, since in 1:11 the issue will be whether or not Job will "curse" God to his face. Job regularly tried to anticipate the possible fall from grace of his family. This action on his part precludes any role that they might have in Job's eventual suffering; he is not suffering for any wrong that his children may have been guilty of. He is scrupulously careful of the honor due to the Lord; the sacred name, *yhwh,* is used only in the beginning, chaps. l–2 and at the end, 42:7–17.

1:6–12. Quite suddenly the scene changes, and the reader is given a glimpse of the events occurring in the heavenly court of *yhwh.* The "Sons of God (Elohim)" are the members of the heavenly court, one of whose functions it is to praise God (Ps 29). They also fulfill certain tasks (e.g., Raphael in Tb 3:17). From Pss 58 and 82 one may infer that they are charged with preserving justice in the world. Hence they came to be called messengers, or "angels." In this divine family is one who is called "the satan," or adversary, a kind of prosecuting attorney, whose function is immediately revealed by his answer to the Lord's (only apparently naive) question: he has been out patrolling the earth. This conversation between the Lord and satan reveals the folk-tale nature of the narrative: the Lord must ask where the satan has been. His mission involves a scrutiny of what is going on down on earth. The Lord takes the initiative in questioning, and one may ask why the example of Job is brought up. Is the Lord boasting about Job, or is he doubtful about Job, whom he calls "my servant," and describes in the same words used when Job was first introduced (v 8; see v 1)? At any rate, the satan is not impressed—implicit in his reply is the wide knowledge of human beings he has acquired in patrolling the world. He refuses to be fooled by them, even by Job; the Lord has made himself an easy mark for earth-dwellers.

The satan then poses a fundamental question of the book, even of life (1:9): "Does Job fear God for nothing?" It is easy to be religious when prosperity and divine protection are attached to it. But what if some adversity comes? The satan even invokes upon himself a curse if Job's loss of his possessions will not cause Job to curse (again, most translations use the euphemism, "bless") God to his face. Somewhat surprisingly, the Lord casually agrees to the horrendous proposal of the satan. The Lord agrees to the proposal, but restricts the test to Job's possessions.

What kind of a God is this? Can there be anything more callous than this treatment of Job's family and possessions? A modern reaction might be that an omniscient and omnipotent God would not find this necessary. God *knows*. Obviously that is not the assumption of the author; despite an air of certainty, God does not know. And that is why the agreement—call it a wager—takes place. By its very nature, human loyalty and love has to be demonstrated, not presumed. That is part of the freedom that God has given to creatures. They can turn rebellious. The Lord does not know their loyalty unless they are tested. Otherwise, the agreement with the satan is a sham; God could not accept such an offer if God knew how it would turn out in the end.

Let us suppose the opposite. Let us suppose that God might turn on the Satan and have recourse to divine omniscience: that would be to ride roughshod over an honest question (1:9). Indeed, would it not suggest that God might be afraid of allowing creatures such an opportunity? Yes, they might blaspheme God to his face. One can be sure only by testing, by suffering. That is the awful paradox. In Prov 3:11–12, the discipline of the Lord is recognized as a sign of divine love. Does God have enough confidence in creatures to give them the opportunity to revolt? All this reasoning may strike us as misdirected or even erroneous, but is it not because we are unwilling to shed our own preconceptions and enter the mind-set of the ancient writer? It is only in being tested that humans can truly show their genuine love of God.

This scene is far from naive. One of the most pertinent responses to it is for the reader to ask, "Why do I serve (love) God?" This gets down to the basics. Bernard of Clairvaux *(On the Love of God)* has analyzed for us what the love of God is. There can be many degrees of love, of course, but he distinguished three basic levels: love of one's self for one's own sake; love of God because we "taste" the sweetness of the Lord (cf. Ps 33:9, Vulg); love of God for God's sake. To complete the circle, he describes how one does not even love oneself except for the sake of God. There is nothing sacrosanct about these "degrees"—human experience teaches us how our love for others can be purified as we pass from infancy to adulthood. But the issue is raised by 1:9 with regard to human love of the divine: What motives are involved in our love of God?

1:13–22. The artificial nature of the narrative is indicated by the rapid succession of the messengers, one on the heels of the other, proclaiming the four catastrophes that strike Job's possessions. There is no reason to question why there is only one escapee from each of the calamities: the Sabean raids, lightning, Chaldean raids, and storm. These culminate in the loss of all Job's possessions, including his children. Job's reaction is famous: "The Lord has given and the Lord has taken away...." He seems to come off better than the God who has afflicted him. He does not question the actions of the Lord, and he knows nothing of the wager with the satan. His faith in God is greater than his undoubted grief. Yet, his reaction seems so mechanical. Is he playing a game? Job's reply seems perfectly sincere and orthodox, since it reflects the common Israelite belief that God is the agent behind everything that happens. The author is careful to note that Job remains without sin in this whole affair.

2:1–8. The second scene in the heavenly court seems to be a mere repetition of the first (2:1–2=1:6–7), but there are subtle differences. A certain tension is in the air. In 2:1b, the satan is no longer one of the pack; he presents himself personally. It is as if Job's resignation to the divine will expressed in 1:21 counted for nothing. Has Job not proved the satan wrong? Yet the Lord brings up the topic of Job again, after the usual amenities ("Where have you come from?" cf. 1:7). He accuses the satan of having incited him against Job "without reason." There is ambiguity in this phrase, which is the same phrase the satan used in 1:9: (Does Job fear God) "without reason"? This can also mean "in vain," as if God is claiming victory in the name of Job over the satan. These possibilities are very teasing, and they seem to be deliberate. They provide an opening for the satan to increase the pressure. He calls for a direct attack on Job's person. The reader is perhaps again shocked by the cavalier attitude with which the Lord accepts this new proposal, as if the trials of chapter 1 were not sufficient. The author shows no hesitation; it may be his way of increasing suspense. We are ignorant of the precise physical disease, but the picture of 2:8 is a sad one that has been immortalized in many art works: Job sitting on the rubbish heap, rubbing his sores.

2:9–10. Job's wife now speaks for the first time, and the import of her words is not clear. She uses the very words of God, "cling to (your) integrity" (cf. 2:3) in a puzzling way. Is she sarcastic in repeating the comfortless words of God? Or is she practical, advising Job that the best way out is to "bless" that is, curse, God, for that will bring about a death that is better than his present situation (thus being, as Alonso Schökel puts it, "an unknowing accomplice of the satan," somewhat in the style of St. Augustine, who called her "the helper of the devil"). Job's reply to her suggests that she is sarcastic; at least he accuses her of folly (the same word is used by the Lord in 42:8 to describe the conduct of the three friends). Job's words reflect the firm biblical belief that God is behind all that happens: see Is 45:6–7. His statement is commonly understood to be a question, implying that both good and evil come from God. Job's reaction seems exemplary, as in chapter 1. There is a difference in the expressions of 1:22 and 2:10. Job now refers to "God" (Elohim) not to *yhwh,* and v 10 permits a certain ambiguity: Job did not sin with his lips—but could he have done so in his heart? However, this seems to be an unnecessary ambiguity; the plain intent of the author is to portray a "saint" who suffers. A holy Job is essential to the strategy of the book, even with its tantalizing ambiguities.

2:11–13. The three friends are described as being from the cities in the desert area of Edom and the southern regions. Like Job, and also Elihu, they are non-Israelites, in keeping with the flavor of international wisdom. Their reaction to Job's sad plight is quite genuine, repeating gestures of grief over one who is as good as dead. So awesome is his suffering that they honor it, weeping and keeping silent for seven days. It has been remarked that their "mistake" was that they ever opened their mouths. Are the seven days of silence pregnant with meaning?

The closure of the second scene in the heavenly court may leave the attentive reader at loose ends. First is the image of Job— a holy man who fears God and avoids evil. That is the judgment of the Lord, no less. Therefore we can hardly speculate about his attitude toward suffering. As a rich and prosperous patriarch, could he have had any thoughts different from his three friends?

The author is not interested in such questions. Job's responses to his affliction in 1:21 and 2:10 have been criticized as flat clichés, lacking in conviction. But such a hypercritical attitude is unnecessary if not mistaken. It is essential for the author to establish that it is a sincere person who is being tested. Second is the image of *yhwh*. Many find it disturbing, to say the least. It is no answer to say that this is just a story, that the events did not occur as described, that this is merely the framework for a dialogue that is going to appear subsequently, or that one should skip to the end and read how generously the Lord treats Job in chapter 42. None of these considerations are to the point. Granted that this book is not a blow-by-blow description of dialogue, whether on earth or in heaven, the Lord comes off badly. The very concept of a divinity who could be so gruff and, to all appearances, so unfeeling is unsettling. Is that the way the Bible conceives of *yhwh*? It is, apparently, one way in which the Bible portrays the Lord—the way chosen by the author, who obviously did not find it a revolting idea. The fact that the Lord is sovereign, the agent behind everything that happens, was accepted by every believing Israelite, as the words of Job in 1:21 and 2:10 imply. And what about Job? Is his response truly faithful, or is he mouthing clichés? We must keep in mind that the author of the book is using Job as a key character in the whole drama. He deliberately portrays Job as a saint, totally attuned to the divine will (1:22; 2:10). I think that we may say that the author has deliberately placed God in a no-win situation. If he goes along with the satan's designs, he comes across as a heartless tyrant. If he refuses the challenge, then there is the lingering doubt: Is God afraid to trust creatures to remain faithful to him? Maybe the satan has a point. What is the quality of the love that humans are supposed to have? Is the "fear of God" (1:1) a servile fear after all? By accepting the challenge, the Lord shows a trust in his creatures. Had he backed down— even in chapter 2, where arguably he should have been satisfied— he would appear to be a divinity who plays it safe and is satisfied with whatever worship is offered. The stakes are admittedly higher in chapter 2. The author is not concerned with presenting any one fixed portrayal of the Lord. He does not have all the answers to the problem of suffering. He is struggling with what may be called the "dark" side of God, which he is so adept at portraying, and he has set the stage for a discussion of the problem of evil and the mystery of suffering.

It is widely thought that the first two chapters find their real continuation in 42:7–17, in which Job is restored and abundantly blessed before he dies, "full of days." It may very well be that an original legend concerning this man portrayed the resolution of the problem in this simple fashion, with Job being rewarded for his fidelity. But can anyone read the intervening chapters, 3–41, and think that the restoration makes everything right? No, the book is not that simple.

3

The First Cycle
of the Dialogue
3:1–14:22

BEFORE BEGINNING THE DIALOGUE, the reader would do well to remember that neither Job nor the friends are aware of what transpired in chapters 1 and 2. They are ignorant of the transaction between the Lord and the satan. The only one who knows this background is the reader of the book! The dilemma rests upon Job and the three, and it will be necessary for the reader to listen to both sides of it, to what the friends have to say as well as to Job's words. It would be only too easy to condemn the friends off-hand, but the author surely does not think that way. He does not set up straw men for Job to knock down. He takes seriously the traditional orthodoxy they represent, and develops it as best he can. There is irony in his treatment, but not caricature. Naturally enough, the reader tends to sympathize with Job because of the events of the first two chapters. Now both the friends and Job must be taken seriously. One should also note, concerning the coming dialogue, that while the friends give lectures, Job complains and attacks them directly, and he also ends most of his speeches with words to God (which the friends never do).

Many interpreters think that Job shared with the friends the assumption about which he will argue in the dialogue: the simple view that God does reward the good and punish the evil. This inference may be true, but not necessary. The principle of "justice" is found throughout the Bible, and it results from the application of human standards of justice to the divinity. Thus it is necessarily deficient. Both the mercy and the justice of God remain mysterious. The working of divine justice is even conceived by some scholars as a mechanical affair, an act-consequence mechanism. A wicked action necessarily brings its own punishment, or as the saying goes, "Whoever digs a pit will fall into it; whoever rolls a stone, it will roll back on him" (Prov. 26:27). The presumption is that the act of digging is hostile and directed against an innocent person. It is clear that such a mind-set does find frequent expression in the Bible. At the same time we must beware of thinking that ancient Israel was always so naive. One does not have to live long before realizing that the wicked do not always fall into the pit that they dig for the downfall of another. Poetic justice is far from being inflexible. The execution of justice (a good act mechanically produces a good effect or reward; a bad act mechanically leads to a bad effect or punishment) is not a fixed order set up by the Lord. There is no reason to deny that such a view existed in the ancient world or that implementation of such justice was even felt to be desirable. But it is matched by many more statements that attribute direct responsibility for events to the Lord. Perhaps both mentalities coexisted.

The attitude of the friends is rigid; the wicked will be punished and the virtuous will be blessed. This is true biblical belief, as one can see in the laments of the psalter (see, for example, the difference between Pss 37 and 73). The connection between sin and suffering was affirmed, but also seriously questioned. The basic mistake of the three friends is to work the principle backward: suffering, interpreted of course as punishment, is seen to point back to sinfulness (cf. the question of the disciples in John 9:2!). Job's attitude is different. He is not about to lecture on divine justice; of course God should not afflict the just. But all that he can see is the divine indifference to him—manifested, it is true, in his suffering—the tormenting absence of God in his life. It is relationship to the Lord that is at issue, not his prosperity. There is no evidence that he shared the view of a mechanical law of justice. If one insists that Job could not think otherwise than his friends before his trial, it is clear that he does not share them in the dialogue. There is a danger here of "historicizing," of interpreting Job as a real person, such as Jeremiah. As was asserted above, Job is not really an historical figure; he is a literary figure—the innocent sufferer. It is fruitless to speculate on what Job's assumptions about retribution might have been. In practice the author and his literary creation may coincide at certain points, but not always. Job is one mouthpiece of the author, who is certainly determined on destroying any rigid view of divine justice. Moreover, Job never asks to have his losses made up and his former status restored. He complains because he cannot understand God's treatment of him, the destruction of his relationship to God. The author/editor of the entire book had no ready answer to the problem of suffering; he simply handled it in the best way he could. The Book of Job can be viewed as the story of transformation of a character, and therefore a live possibility for all. It is certainly not a story simply of one theory of retribution pitted against another, nor the determination of one view as opposed to others. Retribution remains a mystery (cf. Matt. 20:1–16), as does suffering. The author needed a central figure in order to articulate his theology.

Job (3)

3:1–10. This chapter is enough (as if the rest of the dialogue were not!) to tell us how misleading it is to speak of the "patience" of Job. The phrase comes from the Epistle of James, 5:11, who holds out the *hypomonē* of Job as an example. This word normally has the meaning of perseverance, endurance, steadfastness—and that is exactly the right note to strike for a description of Job, because he is not patient. James is right in pointing to the example of Job as encouragement to his readers—

because Job remains steadfast, if also combative. The translation, "patience," goes back at least to the King James version; the Latin Vulgate read *sufferentia*. The notion of suffering is the Latin root *(patior)*, which stands behind the English term, patience.

What may be called the debate or disputation between Job and his three friends has a clear structure almost to the end. Job alternates speaking with each of the three until chapters 26 and 27, when Zophar disappears, and Job seems to speak lines that are more in character with the theology of the friends. But those problems can wait until we arrive at these chapters.

Job begins by exploding in a curse of the day/night of his birth. One can only admire the imagination and ingenuity of the author. The key move is that creation is to be reversed, returned to chaos. The Lord said (Gen. 1:3), "Let there be light"—and Job now retorts, "Let (that day of his birth) be darkness." The succeeding pictures outdo themselves: darkness, gloom, and clouds blot out the day. The picturesque cursing is an art form, as 3:8 suggests when Job invokes the aid of the most proficient spellbinders. They are the ones who can disable the monster of chaos, Leviathan (cf. Ps 104:26), and also the Sea (reading *yam,* the Ugaritic Sea monster, rather than *yom,* or day). Not only the day but also the night is the object of the curses Job hurls. That night is to become as if it did not exist. Paradoxically, night itself is to be enveloped in darkness, as the evening stars stop shining and dawn fails to appear.

It is important to recognize that this curse is not the one that the satan aimed to provoke from Job in the transaction with the Lord in 1:11; 2:5. This is a vivid and dramatic curse of the day of one's birth, akin in spirit if not modeled on the same type of curse by Jeremiah (Jer 20:14–18), and serves to open the dialogue with the three friends.

3:11–26. The curse is followed by a complaint, characterized by the perennial question, "Why?" (vv 11, 20). Job regrets that he was ever born—a most unusual attitude in Israelite thought, where to be is better than not to be, and Sheol (the "residence" of the dead) is the epitome of nonlife (cf. Eccl 9:10, "no action, no thought, no learning, no wisdom in Sheol"). The point is that in comparison with Job's sufferings Sheol would serve as a respite. The poet develops this simple wish in a vivid and powerful way, using the images of one who is stillborn, and a denizen of the nether world along with kings, counselors and nobles. Death is the great leveler; no distinction is made among its adherents, whether they are wicked or otherwise, small or great. The biblical writers employ Sheol in a supple way. The psalmists use the motif of Sheol to move the Lord to act in their behalf *now,* since in Sheol there will be no one to offer praise (Pss 6:6; 30:9, etc.). Sheol is not beyond the divine reach, but there is no *loving* contact with God. Job does not argue thus; he recognizes the pitiful condition of Sheol: should God look for him, there will be no contact possible. Sheol is the place of the shades, or rephaim. In 10:18–22 he returns to the theme of 3:11–19: "Why did you bring me forth from the womb?" The bitterness is sharpened by contrasting the "womb" in 3:10, 12 and 1:21. Job's attitude is extravagant: death is a matter of joy for those who suffer; they yearn for it, as a hidden treasure they search it out. Yes, it is hidden in darkness, in contrast to the light of birth, which "hedged about" those who don't know where they are going (3:20–23). There is a certain irony in that divine hedging; it was protective in 1:9, as the satan pointed out, but here (3:23) it is an obstacle, a barrier to a full life. The poem ends with Job describing his present condition. Food and drink? Only sighs and groans; nothing substantial, not even "the bread of tears" (Ps 42:4). The worst of all his fears (even in the good days, Job had his fears) has come upon him—-no peace, just trouble!

Chapter 3 is remarkable for its portrayal of sheer grief, not only of Job but a grief suggesting all of humanity that is destined for Sheol and realistically cannot count itself exempt from suffering in this life. In comparison with the outbursts to come, the absence of any direct accusation against God is remarkable. There is only the modest mention of God in v 23 and the implied presence in v 20. The religious meaning of the situation will become more evident in the chapters that follow.

Eliphaz (4–5)

4:1–6. In appearance, the reaction of Eliphaz to Job's impassioned curse and plea is strikingly subdued and calm—a lecture style that is meant to give Job some encouragement. The opening words are what the ancients called *captatio benevolentiae,* a kind of soft opening, siren words that are designed to lead Job gently back into more acceptable ways of thinking. The mood is confidential—one sage offering comfort to another by rehearsing traditional wisdom themes. Yet there is a kind of pomposity about Eliphaz. He is the only one of the three to boast of a special vision (a theophany?) that suggests a superior attitude.

In 4:2–5 Eliphaz begins with a certain delicacy, but feels compelled to point out that Job has been a wise counselor in the past, giving support to the weak and stumbling. This is not a historical remembrance. Obviously Eliphaz assumes that Job would have dealt out the same type of "comfort" he is imparting to Job in this crisis. Hence he reminds Job to recall his fear of God and his blamelessness. This is ironic. Job's fear of God and integrity as proclaimed by Eliphaz are not the same qualities that the Lord recognizes in him (cf. 1:1.8; 2:3), even if they are the same words! On the lips of Eliphaz they are a guarantee to Job that the hope engendered by his virtuous life will be honored with divine blessings—of course it is implied that he will give up whatever wickedness, secret or otherwise, that must underlie the present calamity. But there is no direct accusation of Job; that will gradually appear in the cycle of speeches. Verse 6 even points out to Job his "hope" -- that his "blamelessness" (*tam,* the term used by the Lord in 1:1 and 2:3) will in the end be his deliverance.

4:7–11. At least we know what Eliphaz would say to people (such as Job) who are in a crisis, and it is not very comforting: Job could have answered, What blameless person ever perished (v 7)? I know at least one! How can that be the basis of Job's hope? He has not (yet) perished, although his children have been wiped out! Eliphaz will insist on hope (4:6; 5:16); the situation will change for the better. He has recourse to his own experience, ostensibly taking the focus off Job, and describes the fate of the wicked who perish by the divine "breath/spirit" (v 9, which normally gives life; cf. Gen 2:8; Ps 104:30). He then wanders off into comparing the wicked to lions (no less than five different nouns for lion are used) who have no mercy for their victims—but those lions will perish.

4:12–21. Eliphaz has been delivering standard wisdom bromides thus far. Now he turns to an experience of a personal revelation rarely to be found among the sages: a revelation from on high that causes an unusual physical reaction (bones quaking, hair standing up). He hears a voice speaking to him: "Can mortals be righteous as against God?" If not even his servants, the angels, are without fault, what about those whose origins are of clay? Their end is vividly portrayed: crushed like moths, shattered in a day, dying unattended, and without ever attaining wisdom (such as Eliphaz supposedly has).

What is the meaning of this revelation? It contains nothing really new. Verse 17 cannot envision the possibility of mortals being as or even more righteous than God (as some translations render it). Rather, it must mean that the righteousness of God is beyond the comprehension, much less the reach, of any created being. This is one of those "God is wholly other" statements; humans are merely from the dust (v 19). Eliphaz would hardly have needed such a stunning revelation as he describes to voice this commonplace. It is one of those easy theological statements that can serve as a put-down of Job, who should end his wild lament. Or is there another explanation for this question? The reader has been given assurance in chapters 1 and 2 that God deems Job to be blameless and fearing God and avoiding evil. Here is a mortal whose justice is actually greater than the servants or angels of the Lord. Indeed the "holiness" of the "holy ones," who attend the divine throne and are part of the divine family, is never described, but merely asserted in the Old Testament. They must be holy because they are so close to the divinity, but their moral character is not described.

5:1–7. This chapter opens with a derisive challenge to Job to seek an intercessor among the holy ones of the heavenly court.

Eliphaz unwittingly (but the author deliberately) recommends to Job a recourse that will find later echoes in 9:33; 18:19–21; 19:25–27; cf. 23:3–4. Job will yearn for an intercessor and will eventually find one (19:25). Eliphaz seems to imply that Job will not find anyone to turn to; ironically it will be Job upon whom Eliphaz must rely in the end (42:8). He follows this up with a statement about a hotheaded fool (5:2) that has the ring of a proverb, even if there is no parallel in Proverbs (but cf. Prov. 14:30). Indirectly he may be warning Job against the outburst of chapter 3. He proceeds to curse (the text is unsteady here) a typical fool who apparently prospers. His family is affected; they lose their possessions to the hungry and thirsty—an appropriate reversal. But the curse of Eliphaz seems hardly necessary, since he goes on to generalize about the innate evil tendencies of mortals (5:7). They produce wickedness as surely as the "sons of Resheph" (a reference to a mythical Canaanite god of pestilence) fly upward—perhaps a reference to the fever that pestilence inevitably brings on.

5:8–16. Eliphaz has a tendency to get lost in his thoughts. He describes how he would seek out God to lay his case before him—implicitly urging Job to do the same (5:8). Then he spins off in a hymnlike description of a creator who has done wondrous things and will not be fooled by the cunning of crafty mortals, from whose power he will deliver the poor. Another proverb-like statement about hope is offered (5:16); in contrast to 4:5, where Eliphaz recommended to Job that his hope lay in his blamelessness, hope is now centered on the divine will and power.

5:17–27. Eliphaz brings his lengthy discourse to an end with a general beatitude pronounced upon those whom Shaddai (the first appearance of this name, meaning perhaps "the mountain one," or "Almighty" as the Greek renders it) reproves and disciplines. This well known bromide (cf. Ps. 94:12; Prov. 3:11–12) is meant to be consoling: the one who afflicts is also the one who heals. He rattles off a numerical saying (six and six plus one) that indicates Job will not only be preserved from various calamities, but nature will be in a covenant with him—no beasts to fear, no rocks in his fields; in short, a world of paradise, with his home blessed by many descendants. Job himself in this (ultimately deceptive) bliss will have lived a full life when he finally dies. The last verse (27) is in the wisdom style: Job is to "listen" to this wise counsel of Eliphaz.

What is to be made of this discourse? J. G. Janzen has pointed out that Eliphaz has really come down on the side of the satan in the meeting that took place in chapter 1. Humanity is not to be trusted; if heavenly beings cannot be trusted, how much less humans (4:17). However, God's honor is preserved, since there will be punishment for the evil and reward for the virtuous (available even to Job, 5:17–27).

Job (6–7)

The style of the dialogue is rather disconcerting. Job and the friends seem to talk past each other theologically even while attacking each other personally. Behind all of the speakers is an author who has his own logic and subtlety. One even gets the impression that the writer is just as interested in poetic descriptions as in the fundamental disagreement between Job and the friends. Thus, one may characterize 6:2–13 as a kind of soliloquy, the words of Job to the world! Yet they are also destined to impress his friends, although he does not address them directly until 6:21. Verses 14–20 in chapter six are cast in the third person and speak about them. He continues in the same vein as the lament in chapter 3, almost as if the words of Eliphaz went over his head.

6:1–13. Job seeks a comparison in 6:2: his anguish and calamity, on one side of the cosmic scales, are weighed against the sands of the sea. This impossible comparison shows why his lament in 3:11–26 was so strongly worded. He is now the object of the poisoned arrows of the Almighty, whom he mentions explicitly for the first time as his enemy. He defends himself with proverb-like sayings in the form of rhetorical questions. Animals do not complain when they receive appropriate food, but when it is inedible, what can one expect (vv 5–7)? —and Job has been served an inedible dish. So he goes a step further: poisoned arrows, inedible food, and now a death-wish (vv 7–8). For the first time, he explicitly expresses a desire to die. But it is not the same as the "escape," in which he viewed Death as the great leveler in chapter 3. This "hope" (v 8, picking up on the hope mentioned in 4:6, 5:16) for which he longs is to be God's doing, not his own, because suicide is never envisioned. What consolation does Job find in this death-wish? Although the text of 6:10 is difficult to translate, it seems to mean that Job has remained faithful to God's words, and that would be his consolation in death—a kind of death with honor. But has he enough strength for this? Doubts assail him (vv 11–13) . Can he endure honorably all this psychic and physical suffering? His weakness is neatly conveyed by impossible comparisons to stone and bronze.

6:14–21. Job's helplessness does not prevent him from launching into a sharp indictment of the friends. One should expect loyalty from one's friends, even if there be question about the religious stance of the one who suffers (the translation of v 14 is doubtful) . He compares them to the typical desert wadi, flowing during the rainy seasons but arid the rest of the time. One cannot rely on such fickle friends. The description of the wadi is labored and the text uncertain (v 16). The disappointment the friends provide is compared to the misfortunes of caravan travelers in the desert who are deceived by wadis they expected to be life-giving. So also with Job and the friends; he finds them empty and unreliable. They are filled with fear when they see what has happened to him (v 21, of uncertain meaning).

6:22–30. Job taunts them concerning the fact that he has made no demands on their friendship—to share their riches or to incur any danger. Let them show where he has done wrong! There is nothing but words, words! Let them not think that their reproof (v 25) can reduce his claims. He accuses them of being utterly callous, the kind of people who would cast lots over an orphan or barter away a friend. He wants a face to face confrontation, one that is sincere and not theoretical. There can be no room for evasion. Job is supremely confident that there is no wrong on his tongue, that he can discern the iniquity they speak. This is the first very personal attack that Job makes against the friends. The dispute between the participants will gradually heat up until finally Eliphaz will list "sins" of Job (22:5–9). It is part of the verisimilitude of the author's style that these lively and dramatic traits appear so often.

7:1–6. The human condition is the next topic Job takes up— not only humanity in general, but his own particular plight. His description differs from that of Eliphaz, who explained it by the sinfulness of human beings (4:2–7). Job likens it to the slavery that is enforced upon hirelings, even soldiers, and quickly applies it to his own situation: months of misery and nights of torment from a body full of maggots and sores. Inexorably his days go on to the appointed end, "swifter than a weaver's shuttle." This piteous description is leading into a direct appeal from Job, the first time that he calls out to God.

7:7–16. "Remember!" Remember what?—that his life is wind! There is a sequence of sentences about "eyes" (7:7–8). Job's eyes shall never behold happiness; anyone else who looks for him will not see him, and even the divine eyes, looking for him, will not find him. One who goes to Sheol dissipates like a cloud, never to return: "his place knows him no longer" (cf. Ps 103:16). It is quite clear from this and other passages (e.g., 10:21; 14:10–12; 16:22; 17:13–16) that Job has no hope in a future life with God; Sheol is really darkness, nonlife, even if it can serve as a respite from his suffering (3:11–22).

There is an emotional impact from the failure of even the eyes of God to see him (7:8). Yet he also calls upon God to look away from him (7:19; cf. 14:6). The divine gaze is indeed ambiguous, for weal or for woe. In 7:11–12 Job gives full vent to his feelings. His taunt is that God has placed a watch over him, as though he were *Yam* (see the comment on 3:8—the rebellious Sea of chaos) or *tannin,* the Dragon that threatens to upset the creative order. How ridiculous to use the divine power on a mere mortal such as

Job. Let God conserve his strength for real enemies! Instead, Job who is a mere "wind," a "breath" (vv 7, 16), is made the target. Rest asleep in bed? Only nightmares! Strangulation and death are preferable. Once more he adduces his mortality as a motif (a mere "breath") for God to stop afflicting him.

7:17–21. Job returns to his sarcastic attack on God. Yes, he is not the monster of chaos, but he is also more than a mere mortal in so far as the religious tradition of Israel is concerned. The doctrine concerning the exalted status of human beings is presupposed here (cf. Ps 8:4–6, with its mood of astonishment; Ps 144:3). In a deliberate parody of Ps 8, Job is trashing the vision held out by that psalm. Instead of wonderment that God would be so mindful of the mortals created "a little less than the Elohim" (Ps 8:6), Job interprets the divine attention as hostile, overdone, every day, every minute. Let God look away long enough for Job (literally) to swallow his spittle! Besides, how does wrongdoing affect God who is watching over him so intently? Literally, v 20 reads, "I have sinned; what do I do to you?" This might sound like Eliphaz's famous statement about both humans and angels being sinful before God (4:17–18), but Job does not mean it that way; his argument is *dato, non concesso,* "supposing, but not granting your argument." He does not admit to sin (and the reader knows from chapters 1 and 2 that he is upright). He is scoring points against God in the only way he can. Is this the way for God to act in view of the promises of Exod 34:6 so often repeated (e.g., Ps 103:8–13)? God has to be above all that smallness or as Job puts it directly, "Why do you not pardon my iniquity...?" And he adds the tantalizing reason that God will miss him when he is gone, lying in the dust (7:21). Some would consider v 21 as a "mock plea" for forgiveness. He does not really mean it since he denies that he has done any wrong (9:20–21; 12:4:27:2–6; 33:9). In other words, he is taunting God to extend forgiveness before it is too late to right this alleged wrong. God will not be able to reach him (for mercy) in Sheol.

Job's last words are a kind of *ad hominem* (although addressed to God!) argument. Why cannot God let up? Job's putative "sin" is of such little account that the great Shaddai should be able to be easy on Job, who is suffering so radically, and who has so little time left in this world. These are human arguments; they are not an historical description of Job's precise condition, or even a theological assessment. The author of this work is using all the human reasons, groanings, arguments, accusations—the whole range of reactions to the riddle of human suffering in this expression of Job's anguish. Is not that part of the human condition? As David Clines has put it, "In the very act of begging God to desert him he approaches him; the ambivalence in Job's attitude to the presence and absence of God that will be laid bare in the developing drama has already been signalled" (*Job 1–20,* p. 196).

Bildad (8)

8:1–7. One wind (as Job termed the words of the three in 6:26) may be as good as another, but Bildad terms Job's speech a "great wind." With that comes the ponderous question about divine justice and judgment. The way Bildad puts the question in 8:3 leaves room for only one answer. The question is valid, if theoretical, because Job has been disputing the divine justice all along. But Bildad is not very sensitive in his approach to Job's situation. First he casually remarks about the fate of Job's children; they received what was coming to them! And the only way out for Job himself is to pray to God, who will guard him *if* he is just (has Bildad been listening to any of Job's claims?). Verse 7 has the ring of a proverb. His end will be very great indeed, if he takes Bildad's teaching to heart; ironically, 42:7ff. will show that Bildad is so right about Job's end.

8:8–22. What follows is a lecture on the traditional teaching that has been handed down for generations. There is weight in the lessons of the past because behind them stand years of experience, whereas as Bildad picturesquely put it, "We are of yesterday and know nothing, like a shadow our days on earth" (8:9). But perhaps we can rightly invoke Qoheleth on this score: "Don't say, 'How is it that the former days were better than these?'" (Eccl 7:10). The real problem is to interpret experience and tradition together, to allow tradition to be improved in the light of experience. In a rhetorical question, Bildad points out the need of water to grow reed or papyrus (cultivated in Egypt)—so also human beings need God if they are to prosper. The following verses (14–19) are difficult to translate with any certainty, and two general interpretations have been given to them. Bildad continues the description of the hopelessness of those who forget God (v 13)— and vv 16–19 are translated in such a way as to support this view. (Other commentators find a second comparison in vv 16–19, a parable about a second plant that extols the fate of the righteous.) In any case, the conclusion in vv 20–22 assures Job of eventual restoration. In v 20 God is described as evenhanded: the blameless (*tam,* the word used so often of Job! cf. 1:1,8; 2:3) will not be rejected and the wicked will not be supported by God. Job himself will experience a total reversal: joy and laughter—in contrast to the disgrace and devastation of the wicked. (The last word in the Hebrew is "he [the wicked] won't be"—in contrast to the last word of 7:21 where Job says "I won't be.")

Despite the uncertainty in the translation of vv 14–19, Bildad's view contains no novel lessons, except that his theology of retribution is clear and he claims antiquity for it. Like Eliphaz, he does not condemn Job explicitly. Although he refers to Job's talk as a great wind and speaks insensitively of Job's children, he simply exposes the traditional doctrine, playing by the book.

Job (9–10)

9:1–13. Two features should be pointed out immediately. First, Job seems to speak somewhat independently, almost as if the friends were absent, and except for vv 28–31 and the lengthy address of 10:2–22; he speaks in the third person of God. Second, a definite legal tone enters into Job's speech. Bildad had affirmed that God is just; so Job will explore the possibility of a lawsuit with God (9:2–4; 14–21; 28–35).

Job's opening statement is somewhat ambiguous: "I know indeed that it is so." Does this refer to the statement of Bildad in 8:3 that God would not pervert judgment and justice? Or does it refer to 9:2b: mortals cannot enter a legal test with God? The reference is certainly not back to Eliphaz in 4:17a. Although Job's words are almost the same as the platitude uttered by Eliphaz in 4:17a, he has a different issue in mind, closer to the claim of Bildad: Is there a possibility of winning a legal case with God? The language contains many legal expressions, and Job appears to be ruminating aloud, weighing the possibilities, which turn out to be practically nil. He has answered his own question: in the case of a real *trial,* there is no contest—a thousand questions but no answer (v 3, one in a thousand is a typical biblical way of conveying impossible odds; cf. Eccl 7:28). The divine power and cleverness simply rule out any hope of a fair trial. Hence Job's "praise" of the divine power sounds like satire: God overturning mountains (before they know it!); shaking the earth along with the pillars on which it rests. These upheavals are followed by eclipses that darken the sky.

Verses 10-14 confirm the satirical edge of this description. The author is able to demonstrate a knowledge of the various constellations, even if their identity is not certain. The first may be Arcturus, the Bear; the second is Orion (the Hebrew term is "fool"). The third constellation is the seven stars of the Pleiades. The "chambers of the south" are difficult to identify; see also Job 38:31. Verse 10 practically repeats 5:9 in the speech of Eliphaz— another suggestion is that this doxology is meant as irony. Job utters this more in the mood of despair than praise: What can one do with such a formidable opponent?

9:11–19. Job has no chance against a person of such power. God remains remote, not only unseen (after all, no one can see God, Exod 33:20–23), but passing by without even leaving a trace. Nor is there any safety in distance, for were God to grab him, he could put up no resistance. "Who can say to him, 'What are you doing?'" How can he stand before a God who unleashes anger, such as to humble even "the helpers of Rahab?" Rahab is the mythical opponent of God in the battle of creation when God overcame chaos; cf. 26:12; Ps 89:10; Is 51:9. In the Babylonian epic, Tiamat also has her helpers (cf. *ANET,* 67). How then is a legal disputation with such a God even to be thought of? In view of this power and wisdom, and also anger (v 13), a trial is impossible. Job could neither defend himself nor attack with his own arguments.

9:15–24. Even were he in the right, Job could not win the case against such an opponent. He could only plead, but would God listen to his plea? In 9:17 there is a subtle use of the all-important phrase uttered in chapters 1 and 2 by both satan and the Lord: "without cause." Here Job states that God multiplies his wounds "without cause." How true! Even the Lord admits that the satan incited him to destroy Job without cause (2:3; cf. 1:9). Another significant word is *tam,* "blameless," or "integrity" (vv 20–21; see the comment above on 8:20). Verses 15–24 give the impression that the author is deliberately portraying Job as delirious with despair. How can he reply to such a God? Can he believe that God would answer his complaint? His own mouth would condemn him! Or God would prove him wrong. He is innocent but he cannot really know it. It is useless to enter a lawsuit against such an opponent (v 19). Job launches into the most bitter and blasphemous indictment: "It is all one! Therefore I say both the blameless *(tam)* and the wicked he destroys. When a scourge brings sudden death he laughs at the despair of the innocent. The land belongs to the wicked; the eyes of its judges he covers; if it is not he, who then is it?" (9:22–24).

9:25–35. Job turns to the well-worn theme of the transience of human life, but with new and vivid metaphors (a runner, sea skiffs, an eagle). He ruminates again about his personal plight; he will stop complaining and turn his life around. But his agony will not depart: "I know that you will not hold me innocent" (v 28). There is the rub. The suffering is one thing—and serious enough—but the other is Job's relationship to God. That has been destroyed; in the eyes of God, Job is always wrong, as the biting words of vv 30–31 testify: "Were I to wash myself with snow, and cleanse my hands with lye, you would still plunge me into the pit, so that my very clothes would abhor me." If there were only a neutral umpire who could mediate between Job and God—both of them! Job's mind is on the constraints that should be placed upon God (v 34). This is, of course, an impossible dream. There is no such umpire, but it opens up the possibility of desires Job will express in 16:19 and 19:25. This kind of reasoning is typical of Israel's prayer, especially in the psalms, where God is "humanized," as it were, in the effort to reach that merciful divinity, so near and yet so far away. God "is not a man like me, that I can answer him," says Job (9:32). He knows the theological distance, but he will not give up believing in the short distance of heart to heart.

10:1–7. Job turns in direct address to God, even though a legal process against such an implacable adversary is doomed. But he returns to the fray, since he has nothing to lose, so loathsome is life (10:1). He proceeds to direct his questions to God, in the style of the lawsuit that began in 9:2. What are the charges? (10:3). With delightful sarcasm Job takes the initiative. Can the Creator reverse his own creation: "Is it good for you to oppress, to despise the work of your hands, and smile on the plan of the wicked" (10:3)? Then, (10:4), could it be true that God sees and judges just as humans do? This drips with sarcasm, since it is so contrary to the insight claimed for God in 1 Sam 16:7, and marveled at in Ps 139:4–6. Finally (10:6), Is God really so short-lived that he must discover Job's wrongdoing before he dies? Job is not implying any sin on his part; it is just that there must be some pressure on God to be hounding him in this manner. How ungodlike, to be treating Job in this fashion, and Job has no one else to deliver him! What a statement for a human being to make to God: "You know I am not guilty!"

10:8–17. The creative hands of God are taken up again (cf. v 3) by the poet. One can detect a more gentle, pleading, tone in the verses that follow (8–11), only to be succeeded by savage words from Job. There are emotional highs and lows. After all the elaborate care God has employed in the creation of Job (cf. Ps 139:13–16), it is well nigh unthinkable to turn and destroy him. Has God no memory of those intimate moments when humans were created in the divine image? Job, of course, does not refer to the divine image, but the sense of horror is much stronger because he uses metaphor rather than abstract language. He speaks of God's hands, the fashioning from clay, of the divine involvement in the mystery of gestation. Nothing less than "life and love" (v 12) was bestowed upon him, but it was all a crafty design! All along, God was on the watch to catch Job in some kind of sin, and to never let him go: "If I should be wicked, alas for me! If innocent, I cannot hold up my head!" (10:15). God is simply relentless, hunting Job as a lion would. The wondrous power of God (cf. 5:9; 9:10) is exercised against him.

10:18–22. Job returns to themes that he has used before in (3:11–16; 9:25–26): the advantage of the stillborn, the futility and fleeting character of this life. These themes are a preface to the darkness that awaits him in the gloomy land of Sheol. As in his previous speech, Job ends on the note of disappearance in the land of no return.

Many judge these chapters 9–10 to be the most moving of all of Job's speeches. Some general comments deserve attention. They are among the longest pieces in Job's dialogue with the friends. He always out-talks them as regards the number of verses, but he outdoes himself here. Yet only a relatively few lines seem destined for their ears. Job has a broader program in mind; he contemplates a lawsuit in chapter 9 and taunts God with burning questions in chapter 10. The lack of strict logic in the debate is a stroke of genius. Both the freedom with which Job speaks and the wide range of issues he raises heighten the drama. One cannot deny that the author has given the best lines to Job, in contrast to the friends who *never* speak directly to God.

Zophar (11)

11:1–6. The debate is gradually heating up. The first few verses of each speaker will generally consist of personal comments not related to the substantive issues. Zophar obviously finds Job garrulous. Somewhat surprisingly, he castigates Job for claiming that his doctrine is "pure." Job has never made such a statement, but this reaction is typical of the kind of theoretical wisdom Zophar pretends to. His scholastic wisdom has clouded his thought. Job has not been raising speculative questions or holding forth didactic lessons or admonitions in the style of the sages. Purity of doctrine is the least of his concerns; it is rather the goal of the three friends who are bent on maintaining the orthodox line. But Job has said that he is innocent in God's sight (v 4). Zophar is, as it were, pained by Job's lack of wisdom, and he aims to set him right. Hence he invokes divine aid; would that God might speak to Job and reveal "the secrets of wisdom" (11:5–6). Little does he realize that God will speak in chapters 38–42, revealing wisdom, indeed, but not the secrets. Zophar's understanding of this phrase is not made clear by v 6, which is uncertain; perhaps he indicates that there are two sides to wisdom, one of them being forgiveness of iniquity. This would imply that the divine mercy has tempered the divine justice in Job's case; is this an ill-conceived application of Exod 34:6–7? In any case, Zophar does not seem to share in those secrets, for he is is dead wrong in his theorizing, as the reader knows from the events of the prologue.

11:7–12. Theorizing is something at which Zophar excels, and he offers splendid poetic lines about the greatness and mystery of divine wisdom—higher than the heavens and deeper than Sheol. The one concrete datum he affirms is that God knows human beings, especially those who are evil (v 11) and acts accordingly. This statement, true if undistinguished, seems to be supported by a proverb that says literally: "An empty-headed person acquires understanding and [i.e., when] a wild jackass is born a man." This saying suggests something impossible; no understanding will ever be achieved. However, like all such sayings it should not be absolutized; in itself it points to the difficulty mortals have in achieving wisdom. Of course this does not apply to Zophar who is indeed an insensitive man, as the following lines reveal.

11:13–20. He presumes that Job is sinful, and hence he must in mind and gesture (spreading of hands) "remove iniquity; let not sin dwell in your tent." Zophar says nothing about divine forgiveness, but describes in a crass manner the benefits of "removing" sin. Job will forget his misery, dark days will become bright, security and safety will prevail, there will be life and hope. His prestige will be recognized in that people will seek his favor (in 42:7 the three friends will need his favor and intercession!). The last verse is ugly. All that Zophar has promised in the light of Job's repentance is contingent upon his changing his ways (vv 13–14, "if"). Now in v 20, in contrast to the hope held out there, the fate of the wicked (among whom Job is presumed to be) is that "their hope is their last breath."

We have indicated earlier that the author of the book is not trying to caricature the traditional position. It is important to keep that in mind, especially in the delineation of Zophar, whose words may be the least convincing. Yet his views represent part of the traditional orthodox arguments in the face of adversity. Perhaps David Clines makes the best possible case for Zophar: "Picture his position thus: 'Whatever is (suffering, for example), is; and whatever is past (sin, for example) is past. There is no point in crying over spilled milk—nor even spilled blood. It is from the present moment onward that a life of godliness is to be lived, the mind directed in concentrated intention toward God, the hands spread out in an attitude of prayer, and sin henceforth banished from the life (vv 13–14)'" (*Job 1–20,* p. 273).

Job (12–14)

We have heard from everyone, but the debate is far from over. Job will now deliver his longest speech to the Three. Many commentators regard what is called the first "cycle" of speeches as ending with

Zophar (11); others, with Job (12–14) . But the division into cycles is a quite secondary issue. The lines between Job and his friends have been clearly drawn. The reader cannot find a satisfactory "answer" for either party. Is there any hope for the friends? Does Job need some transformation himself? The tension increases throughout the book—a feature that the author-poet was well aware of. We have noticed the rise in temper in the last chapter. Now, for the first time Job's words to his friends will be particularly biting.

12:1–12. The opening lines drip with sarcasm—wisdom will die with them! Job has as much "heart" (i.e., "mind," or wisdom) as they, and he is not inferior to them (12:3b=13:2b) —perhaps aiming at the insulting remark of Zophar in 11:12. Friendship has produced only insult, making Job out as a laughingstock (cf. 6:14). Verses 5–6 are not at all clear. Perhaps they point to the insensitivity shown to those who suffer a calamity; it is taken as a sign of wrongdoing; in the meantime the wicked are at rest. Zophar had invited Job to explore the limits of the universe to see the wisdom of God. In return, Job issues an invitation to listen to lowly creatures (birds, beasts), whose teaching will reveal that the hand of the Lord is behind everything. Verse 9 is unusual in that it is the only time in the speeches that the sacred name occurs. It seems to be a quotation of Is 41:20, although there "the hand of the Lord" is praised. But here Job is working up to a vehement attack on both the friends' philosophy and God's unruly power. The "hand" is found in the next verse also, as an indication of the divine power over life and the living. In v 11 Job serves up a proverbial saying, used also by Elihu in 34:3, that underscores the power of discrimination through a comparison of eating and listening. It is not immediately obvious what point Job is making, except the need to discriminate and discern. This suggests that he is questioning, even denying, the truth of the next verse, which asserts the traditional association of wisdom with age. Job will not accept age as a criterion (nor Elihu, 32:7–8). Instead, he brings up the source of wisdom, God (the "him" of v 13), and he begins a satirical description of the divine wisdom and power. Verse 12 echoes traditional doctrine; see Prov 8:14–15.

12:13–25. At this point one suspects that Job is pulling off a gross deception of the friends (as well as the reader). What is all this discussion about divine wisdom leading up to? Is Job developing the wisdom theme of v 13 only to batter it to pieces in the following lines (12:14–25)? Or are those verses meant as a straightforward description and praise of divine wisdom and strength, as Job has already asserted in 9:5–10? Opinions are divided, but these verses seem to be a savage parody of divine power. The reader can best come to understand vv 13–25 by comparison with 9:5–10 (Job) or 5:9–16 (Eliphaz). By comparison, the wisdom of God as described here by Job seems to have run amok, turning creation into chaos.

Verse 13, which reflects the beneficent qualities attributed to the anointed in Is 11:2, is ironic in view of the description of the destructive action of God, who "tears down" cities and towns especially with irresistible power, and there is no remaking or restoring. The writer does not give specific examples, but the words depict a certain ruthless power. Verse 15 recalls the Flood. The ambivalence of water was evident in the Fertile Crescent. It is necessary and life-giving (Ps 104:10–11), but there are also death-dealing floods. Psalm 107:33–36 describes such a sequence of events, motivated by divine punishment and also by mercy. But here it is a question of autocratic power, affecting both the deceivers and the deceived (v 16). In vv 17–21, the various leaders of society are listed as victims of the divine power: counselors, judges, kings, priests, and princes. No moral motivation is mentioned, only God's sovereign activity, which seems bent on creating confusion and reversal. There is a subtle use of Ps 107:40 in vv 21, 24. In the psalm, this verse is part of a description in vv 39–42 of God's kind providence to the hungry and poor, and contemptuous treatment of the powerful. But in Job 12:21, 24 God's indiscriminate power is at work. Verse 25 even presents a reversal from light to darkness—a theme (Gen 1:3–5) in Job's lament in 3:4–5—as leaders of the people (and hence the people themselves) wander in the dark.

13:1–12. This vicious appraisal of divine power is the fruit of Job's analysis of what he has observed in the world (13:1). His knowledge equals that of the friends (13:2b=12:3b), but of course the manner in which he uses it and the conclusions he draws from it differ greatly from theirs. Seemingly emboldened, Job resolves to continue the lawsuit with God (v 3; cf. chapters 9 and 10). One would think that the failure he admitted in 9:32–35 would discourage him from this, but he is undismayed about his case (13:18). First, however, he must settle a few scores with the friends. They whitewash (God?) with lies; they are quack doctors. He recommends silence as their best show of wisdom (as it were, an echo of Prov 17:28 that if he keeps his mouth shut, the fool can be passed off as a wise person). Now they must listen to him, that is, to the case he is going to put up before God. Thus far they have been simple liars, but they should not be false witnesses in the case that Job is reopening with God. Dare they tell lies for the sake of God (four searing questions in 13:7–8)? If in their secret hearts they show partiality to God, he will turn on them and they will face legal proceedings (vv 10–11), and their arguments will be turned to ashes (v 12). This threat that Job delivers to the friends is an astonishing turn of events, paradoxical, if you will. Job is now defending God's integrity after having bashed him severely in previous chapters (e.g., 9:19–24; 12:13–25). What makes him think that the God who has proved to be indifferent to so many just causes would step in and punish the three friends? This beautiful example of illogical reasoning comes from his heart, not his head. Job taking up God's cause! Doubtless the author speaks here ever more clearly through the mouth of Job. It is also an anticipation of 42:7, where the divine verdict is that the three had not spoken rightly.

13:13–19. Job is really finished with them, although he commands them to be quiet and listen to what he is about to say. To take one's life in one's hand (13:14b) is to risk it; the hand is not an adequate protection; cf. Judg 12:3; 1 Sam 19:5; 28:11. The meaning of v 14a is not obvious, because the image of taking one's flesh in one's teeth is not clear to us. Perhaps the image is that of a wild beast carrying off its prey (Dhorme). In any case, it is clear that Job calls attention to the risk he is taking ("come what may" in v 13b).

One of the most frequently quoted lines from the book is 13:15, rendered in the sense that even were God to slay him, Job would still hope in God. However, the Hebrew is ambiguous. The consonantal text reads "not" (i.e., I have no hope), but the vocalization reads "in/to him" (i.e., I will hope). Commentators are divided about the proper meaning of the line; does Job hope or not? First, Job's hope. What is he hoping for? Vindication from God? But if Job were to be slain, what will the vindication be? This question presumes that Job is rational in his statement. Or is this a dramatic bravado, defying God, a desperate cry comparable to 9:17–21? There is no reference here to hope in a future life. The book provides no evidence that Job believed in a judgment in a next life; just the contrary, as can be seen from many texts, e.g., 14:10–12, 19–20. Moreover, v 18b seems to be against it, for Job says there that he will still argue his case. Job's argument entails fierce accusations against God— can he really hope in God's vindication of him?

In the second view, Job would be saying: God will (or might) slay me; I have no hope. This interpretation is not very satisfactory, either. Job has already wished for death, and in vain (3:20–23; 6:9), in order to escape from his miserable situation. Why should he envision God slaying him now? And has Job really lost hope? He seems never to give up arguing with his God. Again, perhaps there is an opportunity for the author-poet here to play with deliberate ambiguity (see also the comment on 19:25–27).

Although overshadowed by v 15, verse 16 in itself is a remarkable statement, coming from Job. It is clearly defiant, but it has its ambiguities: What does he mean by "this is my salvation"? Merely the fact that he can enter into God's presence (which no impious would ever dare, or ever could)? The salvation, it must be admitted, is not very clear— salvation from death? —that is not in Job's perspective. Perhaps it might stand for his vindication, the acknowledgment by God of his integrity. This may be a case of the author presenting the bright in contrast to the dark side of God.

Verse 17 begins with an appeal to the three to pay attention; Job is now going to focus on the case (v 18a, *mishpat* or "right"), and he knows that justice is on his side. Hence his brave challenge in v 19a: Who can dispute with him? No one, not even God, for he knows he is right —despite his earlier admission that he could not know (9:20–21). If a decision of guilty were ever to be rendered (for him, an impossibility), then he would shut up and die, that is, be silent until death. For Job, life means pleading his case before God. D. Clines points out an irony here: When "Job is worsted by his heavenly interlocutor, he is as good as his word; he lays his hand on his mouth and promises to proceed no further with his lawsuit (40:4–5). But, contrary to his expectation, he does not die: he is restored to full health and vitality" (*Job 1–20,* p. 315).

13:20–27. After the castigation of the friends and the emotional buildup to the presentation of his case, Job finally addresses God and gives his "arguments." They seem anticlimatic. He first specifies two things for God to observe: the divine hand (lest it strike even more severely during the discussion?) and the divine terror (v. 21; cf. 9:34). Now for the judgment! Let God summon him first or he will open the proceedings (despite 9:16), and God can reply. What are the charges (how many times has Job asked for this? cf. 10:2,6). Verse 23 shows that Job is not aware of any wrongdoing, despite a (merely) apparent admission of wrongdoing in v 26. The eternal question, "why?" (3:11, 16, 20; 10:18) reappears. Job moves from a plea for particulars to a lament over the inexplicable divine enmity. There is a pun on his name in v 24b, God treating '*iyyob* (Job) as an '*oyeb* (enemy). God is indicting him with these severe sufferings, although he is a nothing, a leaf driven by the wind. The situation is ridiculous, especially for God, who seems to be out of control. How can God treat Job as an enemy? Could it possibly be for the sins of Job's youth? (13:26). Job is not admitting to any real sins; it is almost as if he were trying to think up an excuse for God. This is another case of *dato, non concesso* (for the sake of argument, but I don't concede that I have sinned; cf. 7:20). Sins of youth (cf. Ps 25:7) might be imputed to Job by God— as a false accusation or, perhaps, as merely a topos of human condition that is not really applicable to God. The divine verdict on Job's character in chapter 1 still stands as an indication of Job's innocence. The metaphor of the "stocks" in v 27 indicates the divine hounding and watching of Job (see 10:14). It is difficult to fit 13:28 into the context, and many commentators transfer it to the first verses of chapter 14, e.g., after v 2. It may, however, be merely a summary statement underscoring the irrational and unrelenting treatment meted out by God (vv 24–27): mortals treated as something rotten, like a moth-eaten garment—a theme that will be continued in the next chapter.

When all is said and done, Job's claim to make his legal case against God does not amount to much. The friends who were admonished to listen carefully (13:17) hardly learned anything new from vv 20–27. At the most, the reader can appreciate Job's courage in approaching God as he does in these verses— again, a courage that is deliberately underscored by the author-poet.

14:1–6. The opening verses are loosely connected with the legal confrontation described in the previous chapter. Only in v 3 is there a reference to legal judgment, and it is sarcastic: will the Lord go to law over such a mortal human being as Job? This is asked against the background of a description of the human condition (cf. 7:1–3; 13:28). Since life is so brief and troublesome, why does God bother? God should be above judging such mortals. The weakness of human nature and the proclivity of humans toward sin is a common biblical topos. This point is being made to induce God to overlook such weak transient characters (v 3). That is a new turn of events, considering the bravado that Job showed in the previous chapter, looking for a confrontation. The argument is similar to 7:19–21, where Job questioned what possible harm he could inflict upon God by his sin. Here the emphasis is on the extreme brevity of life (a matter of divine determination, according to 14:5). Again, it is a case of God overdoing it, of failing to balance things out properly; this resembles also the language of the psalms, as in 6:2–4; 39:40–44; 88:1–9.

Verse 4 is a puzzle, both as to translation and appropriate meaning in context. Literally it may be rendered: "Who will give a clean thing from an unclean? No one." The interpretation is difficult. It is not a reference to what later was termed "original sin." The language is cultic, and the image is used to indicate two opposites, good and evil. It is in line with the question of Eliphaz in 4:17, and also the statement in Ps 51:7: an emphatic underscoring of human moral weakness. In v 6 Job asks God to "look away" and leave mortals alone in order that they can have some joy while they still live. The emphasis is different from the usual idiom of God hiding the face, which may more often be in wrath, for example, Pss 27:9, 30:8. The purpose is that Job might have some respite. He is implicitly pleading for relief for himself, even though he is speaking of humanity in a general sense. Humans are like hirelings (cf. 7:1–2) who have enough trouble in their daily labor.

14:7–22. The rest of the chapter is a remarkable and powerful development in Job's thinking. He starts off modestly, taking an example from plant life. He personifies a tree and asserts that it can have "hope" (v 7, *tiqwah;* this stands in contrast to the same word in v 19). That is to say, even if it is cut down, the tree can grow again. Its shoots will sprout. Its root even may be in the "dust" or apparently dead—but the mere whiff of water is enough to bring it to life. What a contrast with human beings! When they die, where are they? There is hardly any need to answer the question; they are in Sheol, as Job has often mentioned. He goes on to make this explicit, comparing them to water (the very thing whose scent roused the dead tree to life!), to the seas and streams that disappear in drought. The death of mortals is as eternal as the cosmos itself; they shall never rise from their "sleep." Job means this to be permanent, as the reference to the perpetuity of the heaven indicates.

The contrast between the tree (vv 7–9) and mortals (10–12) is suddenly extended in a most unusual direction: "What if...?" The thought of Job turns away from the common lot of human beings to a daring but impossible supposition:

Oh that you would hide me in Sheol
   and conceal me until your anger passes,
      would fix a time for me and then remember me!
If a person dies, will he live again?
   All the days of my drudgery I would wait,
      until my relief should appear.
You would call and I would answer you
   you would long for the work of your hands.
You would surely then count my steps,
   and not keep watching for my sin.
My misdeeds would be sealed up in a pouch;
   You would cover over my iniquity. (14:13–17).

These lines are literally fantastic. They are a tremendous feat of imagination on the part of Job. The fact that he will return to reality in vv 18–22 does not lessen the importance of this impossible dream. Several observations are called for.

1. Verse 13 is reminiscent of 7:21, where Job expressed the thought that the Lord would not find him, and might even notice his absence, but he would be in Sheol. In 14:13 he understands Sheol to be a protection from the wrath of God— God would soon get over the divine pique—and a time would be fixed. A time for what? In this context it could only be a friendly confrontation, for God would *remember* him. It is of course unthinkable that anything like this might occur in Sheol. But the implication is that God would review the situation in a cool and calm manner. This "remember," as so often in the Bible, is a pregnant recall on the part of God; it is not a simple case of overcoming forgetfulness. Rather it means that God will act! One should note that implicitly Job is asking God to hide him from God (appealing to God against God?).

2. Verse 14 is an impossible question, within the context of this impossible perspective that Job is calling up. It gives him an opportunity to express his intense desire for life. Even though this is resuscitation and not resurrection (of which he has no inkling), it remains a remarkable feel for life. And it would be life with

God. It is not a question of restoration of his goods, nor is it a question any longer of a trial. Job would "wait" (one has to remember that the whole passage is conditional) and this is the same verb ("hope") used in that famous passage, 13:15.

3. There is an exceedingly intimate tone in v 15; the initiative begins with God calling for Job; cf.13:22. The divine attitude to "the work" of his hands has turned from rejection to concern. The legal trial seems to have been forgotten.

4. Commentators are divided over the relationship of vv 16–17 to the previous lines. Do they represent Job's return to reality? Or do they continue the solicitous concern of God? Job had complained before (13:27) of God's inspection of Job's steps, and the text of v 16a is not certain. But in 16b the steady watch for any wrongdoing (cf. 10:14) will cease. Paradoxically, God will cover all his sins, sealing them up in a pouch. But Job all along has been denying that he sinned, and asking for an honest accounting from God! Even in 13:23 (cf. 10:14) he is not granting any wrongdoing. There should be nothing to gloss over. Or this may be the cautious Job ("perhaps" his children sinned, 1:5). One must also recognize the deliberately delirious air of these verses, which suggest the unreality of the defiance in 7:20–21.

5. Finally, what is the reality of these verses? Are they merely expressive of an impossible dream? That phrase, which has been used above, does not do justice to the vision itself. Job's aspirations defy what he can really expect. He draws a picture of another side of God that does not rest on some cheap eschatological trick but upon a deep yearning that must have been a mystery to him. However, Job is not able to sustain this vision. When he looks soberly at the hard reality of life, he knows that God destroys human hope of this sort (14:19). The images he uses to underline this are mountains, rocks, water, and erosion. Even the strongest things in nature, such as mountains, and rocks, cannot resist certain inexorable laws. How much more fragile is any human hope? The previous set of images changes now, and the tone is angry: "You prevail once for all against him and he passes

on." The further reference in v 20 to the changing of the human visage seems to refer to the physical deterioration at the approach of death. The human consolation of a successful progeny remains unknown to the denizen of Sheol, who knows nothing (Eccl 9:10). The final verse of this dismal turn of events is an exaggeration. Even the dead (who experience nothing in Sheol according to Eccl 9:10) suffer and mourn for themselves. This is not to be taken literally. It is a personification of the shades, as if they were alive. It simply designates the utter hopelessness of the situation in which Job sees himself. It is almost like saying that the shades do not really know they are dead, so there can be only self-pity left for them. The mind-set of the Old Testament was that Sheol awaited every human being who dies. It was neither punitive nor rewarding; it just was, and there is no speculation as to "what" is in Sheol (for the breath of life returns to God and the flesh corrupts; cf. Eccl 12:7; 2 Sam 12:23). At the conclusion of chapter 14, the question forces itself upon us: how did Job reach this point? How can he challenge God as an implacable enemy in court, and at the same time envision God so intimately in 14:13–17? Such swings in mood bespeak the genius of the author, who betrays a deep knowledge of both faith and despair. Belief and desperation alternate in this book—a sign of how true to life the character of Job is.

4

The Second Cycle
of the Dialogue
15:1–21:34

Eliphaz (15:1–35)

15:1–16. In contrast to the relatively gentle tone of the first speech in chapters 4 and 5, Eliphaz addresses Job roughly, as his two companions will also do. The opening remarks are personal and insulting, reflecting the change of mood. Verses 2–16 are mainly personal attacks on Job, and in vv 17–35, Eliphaz launches into a description of the fate of the wicked. He likes long speeches, as shown by his description of the blessings of the good man at the end of his first intervention (5:17–27). The tone still remains that of the sage but displays no sympathy with the suffering Job.

He characterizes Job's views literally as hot air (v 2), the sirocco that comes off the desert. Job's tirades go far beyond useless talk; they are irreverent. Whereas Eliphaz had paid tribute to Job's "fear" (of God) in 4:6, now he accuses him of destroying that "fear," or piety (v 4). The organs of speech are singled out in vv 5–6: tongue, mouth, lips. Eliphaz seems particularly angry at the impiety of the language he has heard. Job's very sinfulness is at the root of it all; his speech condemns him. In 15:7–8, he challenges Job's wisdom by referring to the impossible: Job cannot be "the first man" nor is he a member of God's privy council ("the sons of God" of chapters 1–2). This seems to be a learned reference to the primeval "adam," who is

46

not mentioned elsewhere in the Bible. Remnants of this alleged myth about the "First Man" occur in the apocryphal literature and it may also be reflected in the description of the King of Tyre in Ezek 28:11–19. Eliphaz chooses to emphasize the knowledge this supposed primal person would have enjoyed. Another trait that seems to support this is the birth before the hills—such as is ascribed to personified Wisdom in Prov 8:22–25 (this will also play a role in the first speech of the Lord to Job in 38:21). The point of both vv 7–8 is the superior knowledge or wisdom of Job, which Eliphaz derides in a sarcastic manner. In v 8 the implication is that one who is part of the group with whom God discusses decisions would have the "inside" knowledge not shared by ordinary mortals. There is the example of Isaiah, who hears the Lord communing with his council in Is 6:8, "Who will go for us?"—to which the prophet eagerly responds. The sarcasm yields to a sober description of the sources of wisdom available to the sages, the old gray-haired members of the tribe. The consolations of God and gentle words (v 11) seem to be a sincere reference to the adequacy of his first speech, which contained a special "revelation" (4:12–21). Obviously, Job's harsh words about God have offended Eliphaz (vv 12–13). Doggedly, he relies on the efficacy of his first speech. So he proceeds to repeat the substance of his comments about humans and holy ones (15:14–15), basing himself upon the original revelation (4:17–18).

15:17–35. Eliphaz remains verbose and pompous. He introduces his message as something he has seen (v 17, in vision?) and has also been narrated by the sages of old. Oddly he reaches far back in history (v 19) to some idyllic past when no strangers were in the land—perhaps an elaborate way of referring to the purity of the tradition, or else the reference escapes us. Now, with this introduction, what is the message of Eliphaz? It is a remarkably abstract and impersonal description of the fate of the wicked. The perspective is this world, of course, and Eliphaz details all the troubles they must face (vv 15–20). This is in striking contrast to his first appeal to Job to have recourse to God (5:8). It is clear that at this point the topos of the fate of the wicked is both an accusation and a warning to Job to be aware of what the future may hold for him. On the whole, however, there are too few traits of the wicked man that one could really apply to Job. No, this is a lecture, and an opportunity for the author-poet to demonstrate his mastery of the topos.

The description of the fate of the wicked person is a catalogue of misfortunes: writhing in torment all his days, even if that life cannot be a long one; terrorized, robbed, enveloped in darkness, facing the sword, wandering, distress (because he defies the Lord; vv 25–26 seem to be an allusion to Job), possessions crumbling, riches gone. Under the image of a short-lived plant (vv 30–33; cf. Bildad's metaphor in 8:11–19), the wicked person will be scorched and withered and never yield fruit. This is a breed that will be sterile—their only offspring, malice and deceit (vv 34–35).

Job 16–17

16:1–6. Job is as little impressed with Eliphaz's discourse as he has been with the other "comforters of trouble," who have only increased his misery and given no comfort despite their original purpose (2:11). He throws back the accusation of "windy" talk (v 3; cf. 15:2); there is no lack of wind, as Elihu's pompous claim (32:18) demonstrates. Their words, intended to be comforting and illuminating, could just as easily be voiced by Job, except that Job's comfort would be real and true. He knows whereof he speaks. But whether he speaks or keeps silent, he achieves nothing in the face of his suffering (v 6).

16:7–17. But Job will speak. He leaves silence far behind in a blistering attack upon God. It is the violence that first holds the attention of the reader: God tearing and ripping and biting; handing Job over to those (his friends) who strike him. God further breaks Job in pieces, taking him by the neck and smashing him. Then he is set up as a target for archers: his kidneys are pierced, his bile spilled on the ground. He breaches Job as one would a wall, and attacks like a warrior (*El gibbor,* "God the Warrior," is an old title: e.g., Ps 24:8). Job is completely undone: clothed in sackcloth, his "horn," that is, pride or strength or glory—his human dignity—in the dust, grief-stricken, with darkness descending upon him. All this has occurred even in the face of Job's nonviolence and sincere prayer (v 17). The savage description of the divine assault remains unsurpassed.

16:18–22. In the final lines of this chapter Job utters some remarkable words. He first delivers an appeal to Earth, personified: cover not my blood! (16:18). The blood of an innocent person who has been violated was considered to be able to live on and intercede with God, calling out for justice, such as the blood of Abel, Gen 4:10; cf. Gen 9:5–6; Ezek 24:7–8. Logically, this presupposes that Job is suffering an unjust death but that his own blood shall cry out (to God in heaven!) in witness. Thus it can be avenged! As long as it remains "uncovered," it cries out to God for Job's (posthumous) vindication. Implicitly he is accusing God of murder. Eliphaz had taunted him in 5:1 that none of the heavenly court would intervene in his favor. But now, even as Job speaks, he knows there is a witness in heaven, a spokesman (read the singular, against the plural of the Hebrew), who will testify to his innocence. Although the Hebrew text is unsteady, Job seems to have recourse to a heavenly intercessor; see 9:33–35, where he yearns for a heavenly arbiter. But the identity of this heavenly witness is not clear. Is it really God, as though Job were appealing to God against God? But since this is a case between God and Job, a third party seems required: a mediating member of the heavenly court. Or could this mediation even be Job's own defense of himself? See also the comment on the "vindicator" in 19:25. Various solutions have been proposed, and no certainty has been achieved. The work of the heavenly witness is described as arbitrating between Job ("a man") and God (v 21).

This great prayer, requesting that God avenge innocent blood, is at the same time an affirmation that somehow there will be successful legal arbitration, an arbitration Job has sought before (9;16; 13:3). Despite the uncertainties in translation and meaning, the passage ranks with 19:25 (a text that bristles with obscurities) as a great act of faith. The fluctuation between tremendous hope and despair is a constant feature in the book. At the end of this appeal, Job returns to the motif of Sheol, which has ended several of his speeches (7:21; 12:20–22). Time is running out and he is on the road of no return, to Sheol.

17:1–5 One cannot take Job's words too literally. Although in 17:1 a passionate outcry indicates that death is immediately to hand, he boldly turns to God and asks that a pledge for him be accepted. It may even be that he intends that God should give surety for him (so the NRSV). Such a move is not unheard of; the psalmist expresses that request, Ps 119:122. But he quickly realizes that there is no one who will be willing to pledge for him. This notion of giving surety for Job appears to be a fanciful thought that passes through Job's mind, only to be rejected. Who would be willing to pledge for him before God, even should God grant this? The metaphor of the pledge derives from a common commercial practice in which an object was given to a creditor as a guarantee of eventual payment of a debt. Job is using this figure to challenge the divine intransigence. But no one will give surety for him—certainly not the friends whose minds have been closed off by God anyway. It is striking that the thought should even enter Job's head, until we remember that it is the author-poet who is creating such possibilities. Are we confronted with another "impossible wish" (cf. 14:14), in which Job conceives the possibility of God giving surety? In obscure verses (17:4-5), Job seems to tell God to have nothing to do with these "friends." He complains how he has become a byword and a shadow. Verses 8–9 seem to be uttered in sarcasm against the friends who are far from "righteous," for he goes on to challenge their wisdom.

17:10–16. Job closes out the chapter with conditions that are not conditions and questions that he cannot answer. The conditions are imaginative and picturesque statements about Sheol as his final home where he beds down in darkness, greeting corruption as "father!" worms as "mother!" and "sister!" Behold his new family! There is no real definition of Sheol in the Old Testament, only many suggestive descriptions such as this one; on another level one can compare Eccl 9:10. The grave, dust, pit, corruption—all rolled into one, these constitute the essence of nonlife, with which Job identifies himself. He began this description in v 13 with an ironic reference to the only "hope" he could expect. Then in v 15 he uses the same word, "hope," twice to indicate how hopeless his situation really is. He and his hope go down into the dust—such ambiguity! Will his hope die with him or be part of his "home?" Probably the former. But Job does not want to die—at least not yet, despite his previous protestations that Sheol would constitute relief from his pain. There is no question but that the author-poet has given the best lines to Job, even if some of these lines are now corrupt beyond restoration. This speech occupies two chapters, but it is one of the shorter ones (38 lines), and also among the most tantalizing.

Bildad (18)

18:1–4. Despite the plural forms in vv 2–3, it seems clear that Bildad is addressing Job directly and with the customary acidity in tone. Job has not accused them of being beasts, but he has told them to learn from them (12:7). Verse 4 denies that God tears up Job (as Job maintained in 16:9). Job is doing that to himself. But not only that. Bildad voices two satirical questions that imply Job is trying to "play God"—to change the world to suit himself. Such at least seems to be suggested by the symbolism of the upheaval of the earth and rock. The questions have a proverbial ring that might be applied to various situations. The moving of the rocks is a repetition of the words of Job in 14:18b.

18:4–21. The meat of Bildad's discourse lies in a description of the fate of the wicked. One may detect an inclusion in vv 4 and 21, in which the word "place" reappears. There is hardly a change in tone from the lecture given in chapter 15 by Eliphaz. Perhaps the description of Bildad is more picturesque: light/darkness, the way and its traps, Death personified, tent and name gone, no survivors, and the solemn ending in 18:21 (often called a "summary appraisal"; cf. the conclusions in 5:27; 8:13; 20:29).

Verse 5 opens with a bromide from traditional wisdom: "the light of the wicked is extinguished"; cf. Prov 13:9b; 20:20b; 24:20b. Darkness is a key symbol for Bildad (cf. vv 6, 18), and in vv 15–16 also Death (Job's only hope for a home, 17:13–15). A vivid imagination is at work in this poem. The way of the wicked is beset with obstacles: six different words are used in vv 8–10 to designate the traps that await them. These are the precursors of Death. But more is to come: terrors, and in v 14 Death is called the "king of terrors," to whom the wicked are brought. Death, personified as *Mot,* a god in Canaanite mythology, is well known from the Ugaritic literature, and there seems to be a reference to him, either as "Death, the First-born," or the "Firstborn of Death" in v 13 (disease of some kind, perhaps). Hebrew thought about Death was considerably influenced by the concepts we know from ancient Ugarit; Sheol and Death came to be conceived not merely as static powers waiting "out there," but dynamic powers that pursued humankind to consume them. This is the background to Bildad's description. The fire and brimstone (=sulphur) destroy family and possessions; cf. the destruction of Dathan and Abiram in Num 16:30–35; Ps 106:17–18. Finally, death means the extinction of the name as well; no progeny is left after them as a perpetuation of memory, vv 17–10. This appalling fate is received with horror by all, even later generations. Such will be the immortality of their name; they will go down in history with no name or memory. The finality of v 21 is extreme: even if their "place" (cf. v 4; 7:10) can be pointed out, it is remembered as the place of one "who knew not God" (v 21).

Job (19)

This is perhaps the most famous chapter in Job, and for the wrong reason: because v 25 is quoted in Handel's *Messiah,* or, shall one better say, misquoted or misunderstood? Be that as it may, this is a stirring chapter, even though Job does not address God directly at any point.

19:1–6. Job begins with a bitter indictment of the friends, picking up the words of Bildad, "how long?" (18:2). Their speeches have crushed him; they have reviled him constantly, "these ten times," as he puts it. If he had sinned, his sin remains with him. This cannot mean that Job is denying the innocence that he has affirmed throughout (9:21; 10:7; 16:17). This is another of his concessions "for the sake of the argument," as in 13:26 and 14:16. In this hypothetical view, Job asks why they are so upset by his (alleged) wrongdoing: how does that affect them? The reason of course is that their safe orthodox theology is threatened by Job's maintaining that he is right. Some would argue that the verb in v 4 means an inadvertent sin, of which Job is not aware. But that is beside the point here; the issue is sin or sinlessness. They accuse Job of sin; the Lord recognizes him as God-fearing and ultimately (42:7) as having spoken rightly. Job's innocence is an essential theme of the book. They have no right to pass judgment. It is God who has wronged Job, not to mention the arrogance and accusations of his friends indicated in v 5.

19:7–20. Job returns to the description of the divine assault that he has detailed before in his reply to Bildad (16:8–14). What follows is a veritable riot of metaphors. No one gives him a hearing. Indeed, there is active hostility. God has barred his way, enveloped him in darkness (cf. 18:18), stripped him of dignity. God demolishes him like a building, uproots him like a tree (without hope for him, although there was for a tree, 14:7). Job is the enemy, the object of divine anger. The battle is so uneven: God's troops —left unspecified, but symbols of all the disasters he has suffered—actually prepare a siege, building up a road that would provide access for battering rams. Against what? Against Job's tent! Again, God appears to be out of control with rage. The military metaphors then give way to a moving description (vv 12–20) of the desolation Job suffers at the hands of his immediate family (v17, wife and children), his servants, acquaintances, and even his closest friends. The

treatment that a sufferer receives from others is a literary topos in
the psalms of lament (e.g. 35:17–25; 41:6–12; 55:13–15), and this
need not be taken as literal description, especially the reference to
wife and children. It is clear that Job is an outcast, rejected by every
class of relative and friend, by every member of society. The translation of v 20 is difficult because normally it is the flesh that clings
to the bones, but the image is similar to Lam 4:8, skin shriveling on
the bones. Similarly, the metaphor in "by/with the skin of my teeth"
is likewise unclear. Teeth of course do not have a covering of skin,
but that has not kept this doubtful rendering from becoming an
expressive proverb—an ironic escape, since Job is barely alive!
What can it mean? Proverbially it has come to mean a narrow
escape, but that does not fit here.

19:21–24. Job's appeal to his friends for mercy is a surprising
and strange turn. Who are his friends? After all the dialogue and
trading of insults, how is one to understand this sudden appeal?
Irony? Or are insults forgotten and passed over in the moment of
crisis? The hand of Eloah (v 21) has been much in evidence as the
source of torment, e.g., 6:9; 10:7; 13:21. Job is barely alive. In the
same breath he can remind them of pursuing him "like God!"
They are not satisfied with his flesh, that is, with slandering him.

Whatever might be the response of the friends, Job envisions
another possible move: to have his word (presumably the details of
his case, or the testimony of vv 25–27) chiseled on rock as a permanent record, lasting long after he has gone. In the previous
verses he had reviewed all his relatives and acquaintances and realized that no adequate and honest memory could be expected from
them. Hence he has recourse to a stone that will perpetuate forever
his side of the case. Many stone inscriptions of antiquity have been
discovered, notably the stele of Hammurabi. Job could not expect
such "immortality," but he would be able to lay out his arguments.
An irony of history! How many even know of Hammurabi?

19:25–27. Somehow Job finds it in himself to appeal to a new
figure, a *go'el,* or Vindicator, someone who will serve as his
champion, vindicating him. This famous term in 19:25 is not to be

understood as "Redeemer," which has a surplus of Christian meaning that does not suit the immediate context. The *go'el* is a person next of kin upon whom certain duties may fall: financial help, avenging a wrong, delivering from slavery, and so forth. The Lord is said to have "redeemed" Israel from slavery to the Egyptians, Exod 6:6; 15:13. In the context of the present chapter some meaning such as "vindicator" is appropriate: Job's integrity will be ultimately affirmed. Moreover, it is introduced by an emphatic "I know (that)," which has occurred several times in a legal context, for example in 9:2, 28.

It is the identity of this vindicator that is a problem for interpreters. Two general solutions have been offered: that he is either God or someone else. What has led up to the affirmation of this vindicator? In 9:33 and 16:19 Job spoke of some sort of intermediary who would support him in his battle with God. He had just finished enumerating the list of friends and relatives who fail him (in addition to the three). He wished at least that his testimony be made eternal by iron and rock. Now in 19:25 he affirms the existence of one who will stand up (in court and testify?). In 33:23–24 Elihu seems to speak of a representative who will intercede with God on behalf of a person. Eliphaz had indicated in 5:1 that none of the "holy ones" in the heavenly court would support Job. Is it one of these that he has in mind? Nonetheless, he affirms that he has a champion, therefore an intermediary, of some kind. This solution fits in with the development that has just been briefly summarized. The second and perhaps more traditional solution is to identify the vindicator with God. The argument against this, of course, is a strong one: basically God has been portrayed throughout as Job's enemy. How can he suddenly claim God as his champion so confidently? Moreover, when the Hebrew text is translated in such a way as to state that Job will rise again (as in the Vulgate version that is influenced by the doctrine of the resurrection of the body), it becomes easier to see the vindicator as God. However, there is no doctrine of resurrection as Christians define it, nor of resuscitation, in 19:25–27.

In all the discussions of this text, one should not lose sight of what is clearly affirmed. Three times there is an emphasis on eyes or seeing. Job asserts that he shall see God (vv 26–27); it will be Job, not some stranger; it will be *his* eyes that will have such a vision. This is uttered not in fear but in confidence, and conveys a sense of being vindicated. It appears to be the answer to Job's inability to encounter God, so vividly described in chapter 23. At the same time, it is a preparation for the theophany of the Lord in 38:1.

The next central issue is to try to understand *how* Job will see God. At this point he seems close to death. The text is not clear. Will this vision be from or apart from his flesh? And *when?* "At the last" this *go'el* will stand on the dust? or is he the Last who will stand? Will Job see from or apart from his flesh? Is this vision before or after death? These questions are inevitable, and they make the understanding of these verses very difficult. Perhaps they are not the questions to ask, or at least, the timing and manner may not be the issues the author was concerned about. But they have been asked by readers, and no ready answer is available. The important point is that a vision of God is affirmed. Any further detail is difficult to specify because the Hebrew text is so ambiguous, if not corrupt. One cannot be certain how the author conceived of Job's vision of God. However, one should anticipate here and mention that Job does see God in the theophany of chapter 38, and in 42:5 there is the climactic line: "and now my eyes have seen you!" When one looks back over the book of Job from that vantage point, it is not to be denied that 19:25–27 is a tremendous affirmation of faith—faith that God will eventually vindicate him. It is as if all Job's complaints are simply buzzing through the air; but this is complaint, not fact. It can be affirmed with certainty that the author-poet never allows Job to give up or to give in, to give up on God or to give in to any accusation of infidelity.

19:28–29. The text of these verses is uncertain, but the general sense seems to be that Job turns his attention to the friends and warns them of the judgment that awaits them. He had already warned them about the danger of lying for the sake of God (13:7-12), so this admonition is not out of order.

Zophar (20)

20:1–4. Although the reader and the traditional understanding of the book may agree that chapter 19 is one of the outstanding statements of Job, one would never know this from the way it is sandwiched in between the speeches of Bildad and Zophar that both plod along with a description of the fate of the wicked person. Zophar claims to have been humiliated (20:3, a reference to Job's warning in 19:29?), and he turns to immemorial tradition, as Eliphaz (15:18–19) and Bildad (8:8) did before him. Indeed, he surpasses them, claiming that his message goes back to the time that humans were placed on earth (and in 15:7 Job was taunted as though he were the "First Man"!).

20:5–29. Zophar's point is simple enough: the happiness of the wicked is brief, indeed fleeting—as fleeting as their very appearance, for they have no visibility; they are like a dream lacking consistency. This is a hoary dogma, one already echoed in Job 8:11–13; 15:29–33. What may be novel is the manner in which this is expressed: disappearance, vanishing. The invisibility is described in terms of disappearance ("Where are they"? v 7; no longer seen; v 9; cf. 7:8). A favorite expression is "place" (v 9b) of the wicked person; it no longer knows him, almost as if he had never been there (cf. 8:18). The comparison in v 7, "like his dung," would suggest stench or perhaps the animal dung used as fuel. The reference to the offspring in v 10 is puzzling; there seems to be some sort of dealing with the poor, but the translation is uncertain. The dust to which he shall be reduced (v 11) may be a deliberate reference to the "dust" on which the vindicator will stand (19:25).

A new world of metaphor is introduced in v 12 and developed at length: evil is the food that ultimately kills; although sweet, it is vomited, or it turns into poison (12–15). The very riches will be disgorged from the stomach of the wicked by God. One image is heaped upon another. The food is compared implicitly to the poison of asps, so that the evildoer is slain by the "tongue of the viper" (v 16). As if all this did not suffice, vv 17–19 describes what the wicked will *not* enjoy. This is in retaliation for their crimes: the oppression and exploitation of the poor. After a general description of the effects of insatiable greed (vv 20–22), Zophar introduces a military metaphor in v 23. Now (24–25) God unleashes the divine wrath to destroy them: "weapons of iron" (probably arrows). The "bronze bow" suggests (bronze-tipped) arrows. These run them through, causing the bellies that were filled to yield up the results of their greed. One would think that the wicked have been adequately punished. But no, more horrors await them: darkness, fire, and the end of their posterity (26–28). This is no ordinary calamity. In an almost eschatological tone, Zophar states that heaven and earth rise to pronounce judgment and, on the day of wrath, a flood. The end of the wicked is marked by the summary appraisal form, "Such is the fate..." (see the comment on 18:21).

This is a lecture, not a conversation with Job. Precisely as lecture, it is as irrelevant to Job's case as are the other statements of the friends (and, in a sense, the speeches of Elihu). Again, this is the author-poet who is demonstrating the broad artistry of the sages. One cannot deny the cleverness of the food turning to poison or the divine arrows (an old metaphor used by Job of himself, 6:4) piercing the wicked. There is no sense in accusing the author of exaggeration, of overdoing it. It is a brilliant display of literary pyrotechnics.

Job (21)

21:1–6. In a sense, it has taken this long for the debate to become formalized. Now for the first time Job speaks—not to God, or in any soliloquy. Indeed, he makes several references to some key words and ideas already expressed in the dialogue. Eliphaz had spoken of the "consolations" of God (13:6). Job would be satisfied with the "consolation" of their listening to him (21:2) and not attempting to "console" him with their empty words (21:34). They fail to realize that his quarrel is basically with God, not with humans (4–6).

21:7–34. The friends have given various descriptions of the unhappy fate of the wicked (8:8–22; 15:17–35; 18:5–21). Job is impatient with this one-sided view. The facts are otherwise: the wicked are blessed! So he launches into a description of the way things actually are. He does not adduce anything really new, but he marshals the data in such a way as to form a stout argument against the friends. The wicked do *not* experience the alleged suffering that wrongdoing is supposed to bring about. Instead the blessings such as those in the Book of Proverbs (and cf. Pss 37 and 73) would allocate to the righteous come to the wicked: prosperity, long life, large family and a resigned, peaceful, descent to Sheol—all this despite their insulting dismissal of El Shaddai (vv 7–15). Verse 16 is obscure. Verse 16a reads: their good fortune is not of their doing ("not in their hand"). But it is hard to forget a connection with v 16b: "the plans of the wicked are distant from me;"—this sounds like the remark of a scandalized reader. In any case, it cannot be in contradiction to what Job has been saying. In vv 17–18 he points out how rare it is that the wicked suffer. The proverbial light of their lamp never goes out, contrary to Prov 13:9; cf. Bildad in 18:5.

An important factor in such a consideration is the theology of collective retribution. Should the wicked be spared adversity (and this was to be recognized only as a possibility), then at least their offspring would feel the weight of the divine punishment. The idea is fairly traditional, e.g., Exod 20:5, but it was also resisted, as the saying in Jer 31:29 and Ezek 18:2 expresses: "The parents have eaten sour grapes and the children's teeth are set on edge." Why should the children suffer for the sins of the parents? Job will have none of it (vv 17–21). Let the guilty be punished directly! If they get off scot-free, why should they worry about the unknown future? One cannot teach God anything; he is the supreme judge. But the fact is that death is the same for all, whether the blessed or the unblessed (vv 22–26). There will be no difference in the treatment accorded the one or the other (cf. Eccl 9:2–6). Job accuses the three friends directly of blindness and/or stupidity; anyone with experience of the real world could have corrected their bias against the obvious prosperity of the wicked who never meet the fate they deserve. In vv 32–33 he seem to deliberately exaggerate the final end of the evildoers. They receive what should be accorded to the virtuous: burial with pomp and circumstance (cf. Eccl 8:10). So much for the vain and absurd "consolation" the friends would hold out to him! It is blasphemous (34).

5

The Third Cycle
of the Dialogue
22:1–31:37

Eliphaz (22)

T HE THIRD APPEARANCE OF ELIPHAZ reminds us that this is
the so-called third cycle of speeches. Because Zophar has
not been given a voice, there are various attempts to recast
several of the following chapters, but there is no consensus on the
rearrangement of verses. Although there is good reason to attempt
a solution to the rearrangement of these chapters, we shall follow
the sequence of the Hebrew text as it stands.

22:1–11. The speech of Eliphaz contrasts with that of chapters
4 and 5. The flurry of hostile rhetorical questions in vv 2–4 raise
some of the previous issues: Job's righteousness, his piety or
"fear" (of God), his integrity. Can any of this, which Eliphaz
hears from Job, profit God? The ironical answer is "yes." It is a
gain for God that Job stays the course! Eliphaz can only conclude
(v 5) that Job is a sinner. This is a sharp reversal from his previous
form where he held out hope (4:6; 5:16) and even suggested that
Job's condition was the "discipline" (5:17) of the Lord. Now he
launches into an accusation of Job's wrongdoing in the style of a
prophet (vv 6–11). Specific sins had not been attributed to Job in
the past chapters. But now Eliphaz names concrete actions and
concludes with a "therefore" of dire punishment. The sins are

social: withholding from the unfortunate what they offered in pledge—presumably their very clothes in clear contravention of Deut 24:10–12; withholding food and water from the needy—an unconscionable act—and ignoring the traditional care for widows and orphans. Job will deny such accusations in chapters 29 and 31. This savage attack on a person whose piety he had acknowledged in 4:6 is not easy to explain, except that the author wishes to illustrate the a priori reasoning that is implicit in the theory of the friends: suffering *must* be accounted for by specific wrongdoing. In vv 11–20 Eliphaz reverts to a more aggressive defense. Picking up perhaps on Job's words in 21:22, he enlarges in vv 13–14; 17, on a traditional claim of the wicked, that God is so far distant from the world, he does not know what is going on (Pss 10:11; 73:11). This vain assertion is answered by the historical record of the wrongdoers, who are punished (vv 15; 20). The enigmatic remark of 21:16b is repeated in v 18b, but it makes more sense on the lips of Eliphaz than elsewhere. In 21–22 there is a sudden appeal to Job to convert. If he does so, El Shaddai will be his joy and forgiveness will be his. In fact, v 30 indicates that Job's intervention will save sinners—how ironic in view of Job's offering sacrifice for the three friends in 42:7–10!

Job (23–24)

Job disdains to reply—to anyone. Chapter 23 is a kind of soliloquy, a meditation on his situation. He is far from entertaining the "conversion" that Eliphaz has just suggested. He expresses once more a desire for a legal trial (vv 4-7), but he cannot find God.

23:1–7. Job once again seeks to have a legal trial, but this time he is surprisingly optimistic, in contrast to the view he expressed about this move in 9:14–20 (cf. also 13:21–17). There, he feared that God would simply overwhelm him. Now (v 7) he is even confident that he will be cleared, The problem is that he cannot find God.

23:7–17. In an imaginative outreach comparable to Ps 139:7–11, he describes a futile search for God. This brings only bitter frustration. God knows where *he* is, the "way" (v 10) that he travels. Moreover, Job boasts that he would emerge from the divine test "pure as gold," for he is in the right path, God's paths, and loyal to him (vv 10–13). Then he lapses back into a mood of despair. He recognizes that God has made up his mind and nothing will change him (v 13). The divine decision has been made, and Job is filled with terror. Verse 17 is difficult to translate, as disparities in translations show. Job either declares that he will not be enveloped in the darkness and gloom of despair, or he wishes that they could envelop him.

24:1–12. Job continues with a complaint about "times." Time is something that is filled with action; "My times are in your (God's) hand," says the psalmist (Ps 31:16). Here it is the time fixed by God for judgment, and Job complains that God has not set up times for his friends to see. Instead, what happens? Exploitation of the poor! He lists a series of instances when God seems to do nothing: the stealing of land by removing the boundary lines; oppression of widows and orphans who have no one to defend their rights; the hungry and naked; those without shelter. The rich do nothing to alleviate the situation, but it is galling to think that God is apparently indifferent (v 12). Murderers, adulterers, and thieves rip society apart (vv 12–15). They operate (vv 13–17) under cover of darkness ("the shadow of death"), "rebels against the light." The rest of the chapter, vv 18–24, is very uncertain, both with regard to translation and interpretation, as a mere glance at the various translations (NAB, NRSV, JB, etc.) will demonstrate. Despite the obscurity of certain verses, Job seems to assert the traditional orthodox theory of the punishment of the wicked. Hence commentators consider the verses to be part of the missing portions of Bildad or Zophar. But again, there is no evidence, nor agreement, on this transposition. Another solution is possible: these lines can be taken as curses uttered by Job against the wicked. That would make sense, and eliminate switching the text. In any case, the passage describes the dire fate of wicked people: they are affected on both land and water, by drought and by Sheol, and their whole life (from womb to worms, v 20) forgotten. Despite their attitude toward the barren woman and the widow, God provides them with security (cf. 21: 13, 32–33). Let them wither and fade away. The final verse announces Job's defiant claim that his words are irrefutable.

Bildad (25)

Bildad's speech is the shortest in the book, and it has given rise to many attempts to rearrange the verses in chapters 24 through 27. Many interpreters consider 26:1–14 (allowing for an interruption by Job in 26:1–4) to be the continuation of 25:1–6. Bildad introduces his theme with a hymn-like statement of God's rule over the sun and stars (his "troops," v 3), but verses 4 to 6 are a tired old song about human sinfulness, a theme already adopted by Eliphaz in 4:17–19 and 15:14–16. The contrast in vv 5–6 between the divine light, before which the moon pales, and the wormy mortals, is quite extreme.

Job (26)

26:1–4. After the customary introduction (v 1), Job addresses a party in the singular; hence, many interpret this as Job interrupting Bildad with a sarcastic reply referring to the mindless meanderings of that character. In any case, this interpretation certainly fits the situation: Bildad has spoken, intending to help and assist Job, supposedly one without power or wisdom—when it is just the opposite. Bildad, not Job, lacks these qualities. Job has previously ridiculed the wisdom of the friends (12:2; 17:10), but v 4 is particularly sharp: where could Bildad have gotten his ideas? Are they really his own, or is his "breath"/"spirit" from another (and is Job suggesting they are from God?).

26:5–14. The transition to v 5 is very sudden; Job (or for many interpreters, this is Bildad continuing 25:1–6) launches into a stirring hymn concerning the creative power of God. As the text stands, it is uttered by Job; cf. also 9:4–10; 12:9–25. What are the "outlines of his ways" (v 14)? These words describe the impressive poem that begins with a mention of the rephaim, or shades, who inhabit Sheol or Abaddon (literally "destruction," a synonym for Sheol), and it continues with the creative activity of God (vv 6–13). This breathless description contains one mythological reference after another. From Zaphon (the North, or the place of divine assembly, known from Ugaritic myths and standing here for the heavenly court), God suspends the earth out in space. The "pillars of heaven" (v 11—we are never told what they rest upon) tremble at the divine rebuke administered to the waters of chaos, personified as the Sea and Rahab (cf. the Sea and Leviathan in 3:8). This easy victory ends with the slaying of the fleeing serpent, a chaos monster resonant with Leviathan in Is 27:1; cf. Ps 104:26. In contrast with other descriptions of creation, even with the Lord's speech in Job 38, this vivid passage leaves much unsaid by its deft use of ancient Near Eastern mythology. It is meant to represent a mere "whisper" of the divine power (v 14). After all, clouds (vv 8–9) keep God hidden; no wonder Job could not see God (23:8–9), but that does not mean that God cannot see through them (22:12–14). One can only revel in this exuberant exaltation of God's creative power. The question that arises is this: what is it doing in the mouth of Job at this point? One can hardly say that it is triggered by the brief words of Bildad on divine rule in 25:2–3. As indicated above (cf. 9:5–10 and 12:10–25), this is not the first time that Job has spoken about the divine power, but those passages are not hymns of praise; they are grudging acknowledgment of dominion of earth and peoples by an imperious and even autocratic deity. This question is made all the more pertinent in view of the next verse, 27:1.

Job (27)

27:1. If Zophar ever spoke in these later chapters, this is his turn. But he has disappeared, and some interpret his absence as a sign that the debate is really over. Instead, it is Job who speaks, and he is introduced by a new formula, repeated also in 29:1: "Job again took up his mashal and said...." *Mashal* or "theme," "discourse," is a rather formal introduction to the striking oaths he is to utter (vv 2–7). Hence, many interpreters infer that the new formula implies that Job's words have been interrupted by passages found elsewhere in these chapters, and that he now resumes speaking.

27:2–6. Solemn oaths abound in the Bible, but none are like Job's in this passage. He swears "As god lives....On the life of the God who has turned aside his right and thus unjustly, he swears an oath affirming his innocence! An oath like this would ordinarily be incomprehensible, but Job is forcing God's hand, at the same time that he affirms a trust in this God. Such is the paradoxical situation in which he finds himself. Logically he can be seen as affirming divine injustice (v 2); there is no falsity in his oath that he is innocent (v 4). In v 5 he affirms his claim to innocence with another oath ("far be it from me" is literally "let it be profane to me"), which expresses that it would be a sacrilege for Job to do otherwise than he has done. This imprecation is strengthened by the statement that until his death Job will maintain his integrity— the same integrity that was acknowledged by the Lord in 1:8; 2:3. The boldness of these verses is more stark and powerful than the purificatory oaths that he will utter in chapter 31. There he invokes punishment upon himself if he has done specific wrongs. But here he dares God to be just.

27:7–23. It is not easy to align the rest of the chapter with Job's stance. In v 12 he speaks of an enemy (in the singular, but hardly God), upon whom he wishes the fate of the unjust. If Job has no hope (17:15; 19:10), surely there can be none for the wicked! (v 8). Shaddai will not hear his appeal. Job returns to the plural in vv 11–12, and he begins to sound like the three friends. He gives them a dose of their own medicine by describing the portion that the wicked will receive from God. Here he mouths the old platitudes that they have uttered at many points about the fate of the unjust. Perhaps it is a parody of Zophar; compare v 13 with 20:29, the ending of Zophar's speech. Verses 14–23 contain little that is really new. There are merely some variations on the punishment of the wicked: their descendants, widows, and riches. What they do not lose will be taken over by the righteous (v 17). The change will be sudden, as it were, overnight (v 19), and a storm wind will do away with the wicked. Other solutions have been proposed for 27:13–23, but are too hypothetical to be detailed here.

? (28)

Chapter 28 is one of the highlights in the book, even if only because it raises more questions than the rest of the chapters. Thus, who is the speaker? Although it follows chapter 27 which, as the text stands, is attributed to Job, there is no sign of continuity between the two chapters. They deal with disparate things: the portion of the wicked person (27), and the place of wisdom (28). Nor is chapter 28 easily related to Job's soliloquy in the following chapters, 29–31. The opening verse of chapter 29 begins with the same words as 27:1, as though Job had not spoken chapter 28. The relationship both forward and backward is so loose that commentators have recourse to various metaphors, describing 28 as an "interlude," or "bridge," or some equivalent. Most simply regard it as a later insertion by the author or another hand.

The topic is a new one: Where is wisdom to be found? (28:12, 20, with two negative replies in vv 13, 21). There is a slight echo of this in Zophar's speech of 11:6–10, in which he speaks of the secrets of wisdom and the mystery of God. But that line of thought is no more than can be duplicated in other parts of the Old Testament (e.g., Is 45:15). The emphasis on the hiddenness of wisdom is astounding and perhaps this is the first development of the theme. The poem in Baruch 3:9–4:4 seems to be derivative. One of the most tantalizing aspects is the clarity with which the question is asked (vv 12, 20), and the obscurity of the replies that are given (vv 23–27; v 28). Yes, one question and two answers! It should also be said that there are some obscure verses in the text, which have prompted a rearrangement of some lines (e.g., the NAB translation). As usual, our comment shall follow the sequence of the Hebrew and the ancient versions. The last verse (28) does seem to lie outside of the poem in vv 1–27, but it is not to be simply disregarded. A consideration of how this chapter fits into the Book of Job will be given after v 28.

The personification of Wisdom as a woman is well known from the Book of Proverbs 1–9, and also from Sirach 24. That does not seem to be true of Job. Wisdom is personified. but it is not described as a woman. *Chokmah* in Hebrew is feminine gender, but personification as a woman is a separate issue. The same phenomenon occurs in the Book of Baruch, 3:9–4:3. This passage is influenced by Job 28, since the question of the place of wisdom is raised in Bar 4:14–15 but her feminine character is not stated. Baruch gives the same answer to the question as in Sirach 24:23. Wisdom is identified with the Law given to Israel. The origin of the personification of Wisdom and the development of this theme in the world of the Old Testament is a disputed question (see R. E. Murphy, *The Tree of Life: An Exploration of Biblical Wisdom Literature* [Second edition; Grand Rapids, Mich.: Eerdmans, 1996] 133–49; 227–29).

28:1–11. The basic structure of the poem is guided by the refrain questions in vv 12 and 20 concerning the location of wisdom. Verses 1–11 portray the ability of human beings to dig deep into the earth for precious minerals. The opening line has a play on the key word of v 12, "place." The poem goes on to describe the industry and the success of human efforts in discovering the secrets of the earth. From their *place* in the rocky earth we have been able to bring forth iron, copper, and precious metals. Although vv 3 and 4 are very unclear, they seem to describe the difficulties of the miners. Verses 7 and 8 speak of a path (to these buried riches) that even sharp-eyed birds and kingsized animals do not know; these lines seem to fit better with the emended reading of the "way" to wisdom in v 13. The steady and rather devastating work of plumbing the earth is described in vv 9–11. The point of this mini-poem is to highlight the ability of mortals to dig out of the earth the most precious items, and wisdom has been frequently compared to these elsewhere in the Bible. Suddenly the key question appears in v 12.

28:12–19. Although the deepest parts of the universe have been explored and yielded riches, "where shall wisdom be found?" Now the true question of the chapter (and of the book?) appears. At first sight, the hiddenness of wisdom seems out of place. The Book of Proverbs is introduced as a source of wisdom (Prov 1:1–6), and human beings are consistently urged to pursue wisdom. It is within their grasp if they apply themselves. True, it is also a gift of God (Prov 2:6), and Agur admits a failure to attain wisdom (Prov 30:1–3). But in Proverbs 8:35, personified Wisdom offers herself to those who will receive her: "Whoever finds me finds life." In Job 28 the biblical emphasis on the availability of wisdom is suddenly reversed and, with it, the pretense of the friends to wisdom (e.g., cf. Job 15:18; 33:33). Now wisdom is portrayed as mystery, only with God, unattainable by human means. The answer to the questions in vv 12, 20 is developed in several ways: first, where wisdom is not: it cannot be seen by "the eyes of all who live" (v 13). The most distant parts of creation have no knowledge of it: the Abyss, the Sea, Abbadon and Death/Sheol (14; 22). It cannot be bought, for it is far more valuable than precious stones (vv 15–19).

28:20–27. The fundamental question again appears. It is perhaps not surprising to find that wisdom is with God (vv 23–27). But this answer is not perfectly clear. Naturally God knows wisdom's "place" (Hebrew *maqom*), and he knows the "way" to it. After all, he sees everything under heaven—a vision that extends to the ends of the earth (v 24). Moreover, when God was engaged in the work of creation he did something with it, put it somewhere after a careful examination (v 27). Three of the four verbs in v 27 are teasing: "saw," "declared" or "counted," "set up" or "established," and "searched out." Just what did God do with Wisdom? The implication is that he put it some place in the world, but where? And how will mortals ever find it, despite their prodigious talents for digging (vv 1–11)? G. von Rad looked to Proverbs 8 for the answer and regarded Wisdom as the mystery of creation, ultimately the "self-revelation of creation." However, Ben Sira seems to provide a better answer to the question when he writes that God poured wisdom out on all his works, and lavished her upon those who love him, namely Israel (cf. Sir 1:9–10; 24:1–27). In other words, wisdom is in this world. God, who knows the "way" to wisdom, put it somewhere. But it cannot be found by mining or digging,

Outside of this poem stands a verse (28) that purports to answer the question. "He (i.e., God) said to man: 'See, the fear of the Lord (*'adonai,* not *yhwh*) is wisdom and to depart from evil is understanding.'" One may very well agree it is an addition to a poem (vv 1–27) that hangs together very nicely, even if v 27 is a somewhat mysterious ending. But v 28 is also an answer to the questions of vv 12, 20. It is a traditional view, associating wisdom with fear of the Lord, and the proper conduct of life that is highlighted in the Book of Proverbs (Prov 1:7). The attitude of v 28 to the poem of vv 1–27 looks like an addition that comes from one who may agree with the mystery of Wisdom as explored there, but then offers the practical conclusion that since there is no way of understanding God's dealings with mortals, it is best to go with the traditional emphasis on fear of the Lord. In the very first sentence of the book (1:1), Job is described as fearing God and avoiding evil (1:1; cf. 1:8; 2:3). If chapter 28 were to be attributed to Job, it might be interpreted as the words of a Job who returns to his mood of resignation as described in chapters 1–2. Such a turnaround, however, is not prepared for, and is very improbable. But then, who speaks chapter 28? It appears to be a new consideration concerning Job's situation: there is no answer to his problem. The only viable solution is to fear the Lord. Verse 28 then would specify the implication of the mystery of wisdom's location with God. The addition of v 28 is from one who wants to answer the theoretical problem of wisdom's "place" by the practical answer of human conduct, the homespun lessons of traditional wisdom. This should not be interpreted as an affirmation of the theology of the three friends, which cannot be reduced to "fear of the Lord." It is an affirmation (by the author/editor) of the faith that appeared in the Job of the prologue, in whom the Lord placed his trust in the wager with the satan.

It will be noticed that we have been speaking of wisdom as "it." Wisdom is personified as having a place that God gave to it. It is not yet Woman Wisdom, the female personification that emerges in Proverbs, Sirach, Baruch, and the Wisdom of Solomon in which her divine origin and qualities emerge. None of that is apparent in Job 28. This chapter raises different questions that we have attempted to confront in the preceding lines. How does it fit into the book as a whole? Who speaks it? It simply could be an independent position taken on the problem. It represents one ingredient in the whole mix of thought in this book. It is certain that the writer of chapter 28 is underscoring the limits of human wisdom concerning retribution. Do we have the wisdom to answer the problem raised by this book? Can we get any further than the first chapter of Job? Indeed, do we have any wisdom after all the dialogue between Job and his friends? That dialogue seems to have run its course without coming to viable conclusions. The friends no longer speak. Job still affirms his integrity, even with the bizarre oaths in 27:2–6.

Now chapter 28 is an oasis of serenity telling the reader to be calm: the divine wisdom is beyond human ability to know. This answer still does not touch a basic question raised by the book: does the world make sense from a moral point of view? And is 28:28 telling the reader to look once again at chapters 1–2, especially 1:1, 8?

More than once we have adverted to the fact that "Job" is not an historical character independent of the author/editor of the book. We mean by "author/editor" that ultimately there is no difference between the two, in the sense that we are interpreting the book as it stands, whatever be the hand(s) that may have inserted later additions such as (many think) chapter 28. As a whole, chapter 28 puts limitations on wisdom, which is God's particular preserve. As with the entire Bible, there are tensions within wisdom, which the extremes within the Book of Job illustrate. The import of this will be all the more clearly appreciated when the reader has reached the end of the book. It does not mean that the hermeneutical problems associated with this masterpiece will then be settled. Extremes are not contradictions; rather, they set limitations for the discussion of mystery.

Job (29–31)

Really, the debate is over. In fact many consider the absence of Zophar as a sign of the end and believe that it is a deliberate omission, for the friends have nothing more to say. Job has stopped talking to his friends but not to God. The friends have disappeared and will make only a silent appearance in the epilogue. What is now left for Job to do? He delivers a soliloquy, summing up his situation, with an eye to whatever court trial he might confront, and for which he had consistently yearned (e.g., chapter 23). He remains defiant to the end. The easiest division is threefold: 29, Job's description of his former life, glorying in it and in his lifestyle; 30, a lament over the present change in his situation; 31, a series of purificatory oaths attesting to his innocence and a final challenge to his God.

29:1–6. As already noted at 27:1, the style of verse 1 suggests an interruption, and that Job is now taking up his discourse, reminiscent of the "good old days." The recollection in vv 2 to 6 has a certain tenderness about it: God's watching, the divine lamp, light prevailing over darkness (contrast the curse of the day in 3:3–4), intimacy with God, the presence of Shaddai. What a contrast to the divine "watching" over him as expressed in 10:14; cf. also 7:12; 13:27! Job is recalling the genuine kindness of God in the days of his prime. No exaggeration is too great to convey his prosperity: steps washed in cream, streams of oil from rock.

29:7–17. The reception given to him at the city gates, the center of the community where decisions were made and judgments passed out, was testimony to the high respect in which he was held! The silence was one of reverence, not fear (vv 7–10). Such approval was merited by his strong social sense for the downtrodden, the poor, the orphan and widow. Indeed he was "eyes to the blind and feet to the lame," v 15. He was clothed in justice, in the sense that he fought for and rescued the oppressed. It is not surprising that he describes in vv 18 to 20, again in highly metaphorical language, how he expected to end his days. He alludes to the myth of the phoenix, the bird that was thought to ever renew its life; he compares himself to a tree ever watered (Ps 1:3), and his "bow" (i.e., strength) ever renewed.

29:21–25. These lines remind one of the earlier (vv 7–11) description of Job's role in the community. Here the emphasis is on the importance of his counsel and speech. Again, the metaphors are extreme: the comparison to rain and reign (23–24). The author seems to be exaggerating Job's role, and the impact is all the greater in view of the statements in the next chapter. The final remark about his role as comforting mourners is surely ironic in view of the failure of his friends to provide that very thing.

30:1–31

In 30:1 there is a transition to the obloquy Job now suffers from the descendants of those whose admiration and even adulation of him were described in the previous chapter. The divisions are indicated by the strong "but now" that occurs in vv 1, 9, 16, and the "surely" in v 23.

30:1–8. Now the tables are turned, and in dramatic fashion. The young ones, presumably the offspring of those who had revered him, now deride him whose smile had cheered their elders (v 1). They are the dregs of society that turn against him in a cruel reversal of the description of chapter 29. One should not "historicize" the description in this chapter, but it is easy to imagine the scorn that would be heaped upon suffering figures by others, themselves outcasts. Misery loves company? In a perverse way, the sight of another who is worse off than oneself can be a catalyst for cruelty; here is an opportunity to lord it over another. Job portrays them (vv 2–7) in terms reminiscent of his description of wretched people in 24:5–12. They themselves are outcasts, perhaps on the same despicable level as that of Job, but he detests them as contemptible.

29:9–15. It is difficult for the modern reader to appreciate the opprobrium attached to one who has been abandoned by God (cf. Ps 22:2; Is 53:4b). But the Bible is full of such examples: suffering is a sign of sin, of divine disfavor. This belief undergirds the vivid portrayal of the treatment meted out to Job. He is scum, worthy of their spit. Although God is not mentioned, it is clear that he is responsible for the calamities and indignities that befall Job; the imagery is reminiscent of the warlike actions of God against Job in 16:8–14; cf. 19:8–12.

30:16–31. Day and night Job's physical sufferings continue; v 18 is uncertain, but he seems to ascribe his troubles to divine initiative, so that in v 20 he appeals to God; he has not done this since 17:3–4. The language is typical of the laments found in the psalter, e.g., Ps 22:2–3. God is killing him (v 23), reducing him to "dust and ashes" (cf. Job 10:9). The blessings that the faithful could expect disappear in darkness and misery (vv 26–28). He is condemned to be ostracized—as the biblical language puts it so vividly, "the brother of jackals." The total reversal is expressed metaphorically by the "pipe" and "lyre" —these instruments will sound notes of mourning, not rejoicing.

31:1–40

Suddenly there appears a series of imprecatory oaths. These seem to be imitations of the negative confessions of Egyptian funerary texts; the paintings accompanying these texts portray the judgment:

the weighing of the heart of the dead person on the scales of truth. The full form is to be found in vv. 7–8; 9–10; 21–22; and 38–40. The formula is, "If I have done such and such (the particular crime), let such and such (the punishment) be done to me." Sometimes only the first half is mentioned, and the punishment is taken for granted without being indicated. This short oath can be seen in vv 5, 13, 16, 19, 24, 25, 29, 31, and 33. There is some uncertainty about the number of such imprecations Job calls down upon himself. Commentators vary in counting between nine and sixteen, because some confessions can be joined together as a unit.

More important than the mere oaths and their number is the question, why is this style adopted here? It underlines the righteousness of Job in a striking way; it is more emphatic than his previous avowals of sinlessness. Thus it is in keeping with the bravado toward God that he has demonstrated. Although it is not modeled on the Decalogue, the list indicates important points of morality, especially social relationship. Perhaps too it describes an ethical ideal that the author wanted to spell out for his readers. In any case, it provides a closure that challenges God to act. It might be noted that both the beginning and ending are abrupt. That is to say, the opening verse begins with an affirmation (not an oath) that Job has not lusted after a woman. The ending (vv 38–40) is merely one of the many oaths, and seems anticlimactic after the stirring challenge in vv 35-37. But there is no escaping the impact of this chapter. Job is appealing to God against God!

31:1–4. Verse 1 is a flat denial of adultery, both in act and also in desire (expressed very forcefully by the act of covenanting). This goes beyond the legislation laid out in Deut 22:22–30. The following verses are probably all rhetorical questions that assume the justice of God: correct moral judgment, punishing evildoers and caring for the virtuous, divine supervision and standards set for the morality of humankind.

31:5–8. This oath, formulated only implicitly, begins with another rhetorical question, and Job asserts his integrity, and rejection of deceit under the image of being weighed on scales and thus tested by God. In Prov 24:12 God probes the human heart, but the scales of v 6 probably refer to practical business dealings. What applies to just transactions on earth should also apply to God; cf. Prov 20:10. Verses 7-8 are a clear and unambiguous example of the oath formula. Probably the sowing/reaping (v 8) is a metaphor for requital. In this case Job's integrity is described in metaphors of feet, heart, eye, and hands—commonly used in wisdom discourse, as in Prov 4:21–27.

31:9–12. Adultery is expressed here with euphemisms ("door," "grind," "kneel"); it is rejected under the penalty of having his wife belong to another—a very sexist statement that flows from the tenth commandment that the wife is the property of the husband. A type of talion law is assumed here. The horror at adultery is expressed vividly in v 12, and the divine wrath is described in Deut 32:22.

31:13–15. Job's treatment of his slaves is in line with the ideals of the sages (both have one Maker; cf. Prov 17:5; 22:2), but Job goes beyond this by recognizing the *mishpat* or right of a slave. Otherwise he could not face God. This is also a reminder how the Lord failed to have regard for "my servant/slave," namely Job cf. 1:8, and 7:1–2; 14:6.

31:16–20. Job's social sensitivity is displayed in a series of oaths. First, the poor, that is, preeminently the widow and orphan, with whom he shared his food. From his "mother's womb," in other words, all his life, he was a guide to the widow. Similarly with the destitute in need of clothing—his care for them is expressed in vivid terms in vv 19–20.

31:21–23. Job's treatment of the fatherless is exemplary, but the details are unclear. The import of raising his "hand" (usually a symbol of power), and the role of his helpers in the gate are difficult to determine. The punishment (22) is expressed by the talion law; his own physical arm is to fall off. He is motivated in this by the terror of God.

31:24–25. The conditional sentences (they can also be construed as rhetorical questions that are to be denied) deal with riches and wealth—a suspicion about Job that had been voiced by

Eliphaz (cf. 22:24–25). Riches can never be a source of human security (e.g., Ps 49:6–8)—only God.

31:26–28. Neither could Job be seduced by the sun (literally, "light") and moon, or make any ritual gesture of kissing the hand. The veneration of heavenly bodies as deities was common in the ancient world. For Job, such actions would be idolatry. Reliance upon riches and idolatry seem to be included in one condemnation (v 28).

31:29–30. Leviticus 19:17 forbade vengeance and vindictiveness, at least within the community, and this was also a wisdom ideal, as seen in Prov 20:22 and 24:17–19. But there is frequent expression of joy at the downfall of enemies, or *Schadenfreude,* especially in the psalter (e.g., 52:8–12); in general there is the attitude that the just will rejoice at the downfall of the wicked.

31:31–32. Hospitality is clearly the theme of v 32, although v 31 is obscure, either recording praise of Job's generosity or expressing hostility against outsiders. Hospitality was normally a binding virtue, but it could be neglected in the case of strangers.

31:33–34. Finally, Job was not hypocritical about his "iniquity" by attempting to hide it; the opinion of others did not govern his conduct. This last admission is not easy to explain. Has the author included it as a sign of Job's openness and integrity, without really adverting to the implications for the sinless Job that he has portrayed? In other words, this could be a standard "negative confession" that a sincere person would make, and this admission is simply included here, even if not strictly applicable to Job. It is almost as if wrongdoing is not the issue, but rather his openness and honesty before others. It is useless to quibble about sinlessness in view of the divine judgment in 1:8; 2–3.

31:35–37. With great panache, Job issues a final word to Shaddai: "Here is my *tau*" (the final letter of the Hebrew alphabet— which can be interpreted as his signature or final statement). If there is to be a response, it could only be a pronouncement of Job's innocence, which he would wear as an epaulet, a turban. N. Habel has described well the irony of this scene: "In short, Job will remind God of that which God has spent years observing. Job will parade his perfection before God's face as if God has forgotten Job's ways." As mentioned before, vv 38–40 seem anticlimactic, but perhaps they can be defended in the light of the importance of the land in Israelite thought. If Job has exploited it and the tenants who were entitled to the produce, then let that land (personified!) cry out against him and be rendered sterile, yielding no profit for Job.

Job's soliloquy in chapters 29–31 is signed with the remark in 31:40c that "the words of Job are ended." J. G. Janzen has pointed out the neat ambiguity in the translation of the Hebrew word for "ended"; it can also mean completed in a moral sense, designating one who is so characterized by the Lord in 1:1,8; 2:3,9. Job's words are at an end; he has only a few lines left in the book (40:4–5; 42:2–6). At this point we expect that the Lord would rise to Job's stout challenge. But no, we are confronted by a young sage, Elihu.

6

Elihu
32:1–37:24

The Sudden Appearance of Elihu

MANY THEORIES HAVE BEEN ADVANCED to explain the sudden intervention of Elihu, who gives the appearance of being a bystander, even one who has taken notes on the dialogue. But he surely has not listened to the warning given in chapter 28; he has no doubt about his own wisdom, although at the end he seems to yield to the mystery of Shaddai (37:23–24). We will leave to the end of his speeches a discussion of how he fits into the book. The best approach is to take Elihu for what he is and add him to the mix. Elihu's four speeches are: 32:6–33:33; 34:1–37; 35:1–16; 36:1–37:24.

32:1–5. The introduction of Elihu is not auspicious; when he begins to speak (v 6), he does so in a bombastic style, filled with his own importance and angry with everyone except himself. But this judgment may be too subjective. Did the ancients read him that way? "Angry" he surely is; no less than four times is this mentioned in five verses. He is introduced with an Israelite identity; his name means "he [presumably *yhwh*] is my God," and his father's name means "El blesses." He is given the honor of belonging to the family of Buz, who according to Gen 22:20–21 was a nephew of Abraham and a brother of Uz, the area that Job came from. The "family of Ram" is associated with Judah and David. Hence there seems to be a deliberate identification of him as an Israelite He is angered first by the silence of the friends, who say nothing more to Job. The reason for their silence is that Job is "righteous in his own eyes." That happens to be true in fact, but the phrase has a specific nuance in wisdom circles. A judgment "in one's own eyes" is always suspect. Thus Prov 26:12, "You see one wise in his own eyes? There is more hope for a fool than for him"; cf. Prov 12:15; 28:11. So the three shut up, since Job is the classical incorrigible fool in their view. Elihu is angry at Job because he claims to be right against God. He is angry at the friends because they had not really answered Job but condemned him. However, the reference to Job at the end of v 3 is a rare case of a "correction of the scribes," an ancient if infrequent practice in Jewish tradition. Originally the text read "God" instead of "Job," and hence it would have indicated that God, not Job, was in the wrong, or condemned. Verse 4, concerning Elihu's patient silence, anticipates vv 6–10: age has the edge over youth in the matter of wisdom. But it turns out that this is really another reason for anger; the three have nothing to reply.

Elihu's First Speech (32:6–33:33)

32:6–10. Verses 6–7 sound terribly deferential, but they may be so only for modern ears. After all, Elihu has a barrier to overcome, his youth. It is true to life that one did not just barge into a discussion among elders. However, he answers this difficulty with "the spirit of Shaddai" (v 8). This is not the ordinary life-breath; it is a gift of God that enables a person to impart wisdom; cf. Is 11:2, and in Prov 2:6, wisdom is a "gift" of the Lord.

32:11–16. An inclusion for these verses is indicated by the repetition of "wait." But Elihu can wait no longer. He has paid scrupulous attention to the argumentation, but is convinced that the three have failed, that they believe only God can answer Job.

32:17–22. Elihu compares his compulsion to speak to a wineskin ready to burst from its fermentation (vv 18–19). So he will vanquish Job's arguments. Is this an appropriate or merely a bombastic metaphor? His claim to be fair and impartial is put under the authority of his Maker, who would do away with him, should he fail to be even-handed; however, it will appear that he does show partiality—for God. Elihu makes some risky statements after the question raised in chapter 28 about the place of wisdom. Yet he plunges forward lest the three friends yield and say "we have found wisdom" (v 13; cf. 28:12, 20) in Job's words. His verbosity spills into 33:1–7, so that his first speech, 32:6–33:33, does not really get going until 32:8.

33:1–7. In the style of a typical wisdom teacher, he appeals to Job to "listen" (e.g., Prov 2:1–3; 4:1–2). In vv 3–4 he seems to regard himself in a special way, as formed by the spirit of God. He is hardly on the same level as Job, despite what he says about their equality in vv 6–7. Job has nothing to fear; he is being told: "Answer me, if you can" (v 5). It soon becomes evident that no space will be allotted to Job to answer this garrulous person.

33:8–12. Elihu sums up Job's statements on two levels: 1) claims to innocence in v 9, which can be seen often and clearly in 9:21; 10:7; 23:10–11; 27:5–6, and in all of chapter 31; and 2) accusations of punishing treatment, which resemble very closely 13:24, 27. His reply to this is not enlightening: "God is greater than man" (v 12), for Job has also made the same point, bitterly, in 9:4–21. Hence Elihu's general conclusion is really wide of the mark. Although he has paid attention to Job's complaints, as the above texts indicate, he has not listened with sympathy.

33:13–28. Job's complaint that God does not answer him is simply mistaken. God *does* answer, and in two ways, by dreams (14–18) and by sickness (19–22). The dreams and visions Job had received were frightening (7:14), but Elihu claims that God is thereby acting to influence human conduct and put down human pride (vv 16–17). Thus there is a happy ending; he is delivered from the "pit" (=Sheol, and it occurs five times in the chapter). Elihu seems to gloss over the struggle that presumably is involved in this conversion; it is presumed that the dream/vision has effected a change. The second "answer" from God is described vividly in 19-22, and it would seem appropriate to Job's condition. But is this punishment or not? Verse 30 will indicate that it is medicinal or curative. At this point (v 23) Elihu calls on the saving intervention of an intermediary or arbiter (the same term used by Job in 16:20). The description of the work of this heavenly mediator is not clear; he seems to declare the sinner just, and to imply that he has found a ransom for him. The ransom is left unspecified, but the confession of sin is clear in v 27. In the style of a typical thanksgiving psalm, the converted sinner admits wrongdoing and goes on to acknowledge deliverance. The reader cannot but feel that this theology is simply not to the point. Job was not a sinner needing conversion.

33:29–33. Elihu concludes his speech almost lightheartedly in vv 29–30—such is the way God operates, as Elihu understands it. The challenge to Job to listen, to speak, to be silent and learn wisdom, is a throwback to vv 1–3. He does not give (that is, the author does not provide) an opportunity to Job to say a word. What would the modern reader say at this point?

Elihu's Second Speech (34:1–37)

Here Elihu almost loses sight of Job and his predicament, except for vv 33ff.; he addresses the wise men in particular (vv 2, 10, 34). Presumably these would be the three friends, with whom he had already become so angry. He then proceeds to enlarge on the integrity of the divine actions.

34:1–9. An appeal to the "wise" to listen is followed by a proverb used already by Job in 12:11, "The ear tests words as the palate tastes food." Elihu seems to be co-opting any bystander who would want to be considered wise: *We* shall determine what is truly right (*mishpat,* used six times throughout his speech). His quotation of Job in 5-6 is based on 27:2; 9:20, and the "arrows" are those of 6:4. He goes on to associate Job's views with those of evildoers.

34:10–37. Elihu's arguments are very abstract. He takes an oath (v 10) on Shaddai's justice. God cannot do wrong, or pervert *mishpat* (12), since he is supremely sovereign and regulates the whole world. Should he take back his breath, that is the end of all life, vv 14–15; cf. Ps 104: 29–30; Eccl 12:7. Hence the traditional retribution doctrine is enunciated in v 11. Of course that doctrine is precisely what is at issue, and Elihu seems to be skirting it with his obscure philosophy.

He stops to catch his breath and address another appeal, but in the singular (v 16). Again, his argument fails to face the hard facts. Of course, no one can condemn "the Just, Mighty One" (17), and he illustrates this from the divine treatment of rulers (18–20). Moreover, God sees everything, even the darkest places, and overturns the mighty and the wicked. And he hears the cry of the poor and afflicted, despite Job's denial in 24:1–12. All this is asserted as matter of fact, not subject to dispute.

The text in vv 29–37 is obscure; translations differ widely, none of them certain, and hence there are varying interpretations. In any case, Elihu has not let up in his lecturing to Job, nor his judgment on Job's conduct. Verses 35–37 make that clear.

Elihu's Third Speech (35:1–16)

This is the shortest of his speeches, and takes up two problems: 1) What gain is there in not sinning (v 3b)? and 2) God does not hear the cry of the oppressed (e.g., v 14b).

35:1–8. Elihu begins aggressively, referring back to Job's claim in 34:5 to be in the "right" (again, *mishpat*), as opposed to God, and he alleges that Job denies any advantage in being good—apparently an interpretation; cf. 34:9. But the answer that is given to Job is as airy as the invitation in v 5 to behold the skies above. The reasons are strange: sin cannot affect God, nor does righteousness provide him with anything—only one's neighbor is affected by good or evil conduct (vv 6–7). Apparently Elihu did not hear Job's question in 7:20, which taunted God about how his "sin" affected God.

35:9–16. The second argument begins by describing a concrete situation: the oppressed cry out to God but God does not respond. Why? Elihu points in v 12b to human pride as the reason. It would appear that prayer, not outcry or rage, which characterizes Job's utterances, is what truly captures the Lord's attention (the meaning of the text in vv 13–15 is murky). The final jab at Job, "words without knowledge," v 16, anticipates the accusation of the Lord in 38:2.

Elihu's Fourth Speech (36:1–37:24)

This consists clearly of two parts: 36:1–21, which describes God's dealings with human beings, and 36:22–37:24, a hymnlike celebration of divine power and majesty.

36:1–4. These introductory remarks are addressed to Job, but they do not delve into the details of what Job has said. Elihu's purpose is to say a little more about his "Maker." He has not lost the superior tone that he first adopted; he describes himself as "perfect in knowledge," and this is a knowledge that is "from afar" (v 3). Perhaps this refers to that distant God, who knows where wisdom is (28:23). Elihu has already laid claim to the wisdom that comes from the spirit of Shaddai (32:7–8). He is convinced not only of the justice of God, but of his own ability to demonstrate it.

36:5–15. From his premise that God is powerful, knowing, and just (vv 5–6), Elihu moves on to show that God exalts the righteous, raising them to the levels of royalty (v 7). But this does not mean they are without trials, which God uses to show up their wrongdoing and prepare them for conversion. If they listen to his *musar* (discipline, instruction) and turn from their sins, then good and pleasant years are ahead of them. But they shall perish if they do not listen (vv 8–12). Elihu's views are not new; they reflect the doctrine he has preached in chapter 33, the use of affliction or suffering in turning sinners to God. Again, there is the rub. Job, because of his integrity, cannot connive in falsehood. Elihu goes on to describe the hapless fate of the "godless of heart" (vv 13–14). Unlike the oppressed, they did not learn from their affliction. It is not clear why he associates their premature death to that of prostitutes in v 14.

36:16–21. This portion of the chapter is poorly preserved, and various translations have been advanced. Little is to be gained by commenting on uncertainty. It is not even clear that the next unit begins with v 22, but the reference to God and the divine power suggests that a new topic is being introduced. Hence the following passage, 36:22–37:24, can be regarded as Elihu's final word.

36:22–36:24. These verses clearly contain a hymn, which is sandwiched between two appeals to Job. The imperatives in 22–25 indicate questions directed to him, and the ending in 37:14–24 is likewise addressed to him (has the reader noticed that Elihu is the only one to address Job by name?).

36:22–25. These verses serve as an introduction to the hymn. They recall God as powerful and as teacher; one may compare v 23 with Is 40:13–14: "Who has directed the spirit of the Lord, or taught him as counselor….Who taught him the path to justice...?" The rhetorical questions can be seen as a warning to Job. He is told to remember, to recall the divine works in praise, such as he was probably wont to do—to react like all who have seen and sung about them.

36:26–37:13. In some respects this hymn anticipates words and ideas that will appear in the Lord's speech in chapter 38, and many interpret this final speech of Elihu as a lead-in to the theophany that will be described next. It can be considered a development of the affirmation of divine power in 36:5. In a general way Elihu surveys a number of meteorological phenomena: clouds, lightning, thunder, storm, snow, cold, frost, hail—all this functioning at the divine command, whether for correction or for mercy (37:13). He is using these phenomena to prove the intelligent power of God, which also works for sapiential purposes. We are not sufficiently aware of the way in which the ancients conceived of the universe, especially when it is described with poetic imagination. In vv 27–28 rainfall seems to be described as resulting from a cycle of evaporation and fall. Moreover, it varies, in drops or in torrents. There is much we do not know, such as the pavilions from which issues the divine thunder, and also lightning, to uncover the roots of the sea (vv 29–30). In all this he "judges" or controls peoples by the food he provides, and also by the lightning that he employs (31–32). Elihu lingers over the topic of thunder and lightning (37:1–5), which fascinated the ancients; cf. Ps 29 for "the voice of the Lord." The rainy season also produced snow, especially in the higher altitudes; the white-capped Mt. Hermon stays visible for a long period. Again, this fascinated people; cf. Ps 147:16 ("snow like wool, frost like ashes"). God's creatures seek a safe haven while the tempest comes, fulfilling God's double purpose, either to punish or show favor (vv 6–13).

If Elihu appeared to wander in his description of "the marvels of God," he did not forget his target. In a series of rhetorical questions, 37:14–18, that resemble those of the Lord in chapter 38, he taunts Job for his ignorance and impotence of these "marvels," which he continues to describe. Apparently all this is supposed to reduce Job to silence—at any rate, nowhere in the book does Job ever take any notice of Elihu. It is interesting to note that Elihu describes God as "perfect in knowledge," the very phrase that he used to characterize himself in 36:4! He ends his discourse with a flourish. Just as one cannot gaze into the sun, so one cannot look upon God (or death will ensue—a common biblical idea), so great is his splendor. Finally, there is his power and righteousness—here he turns back to the ideas with which he began, in 36:5; but he ends on the traditional note of fearing God.

In 37:23 Elihu states that we cannot discover Shaddai—this almost at the moment when the Lord will make the sudden appearance in 38:1. In the same way, he says (37:24) that one should fear God, since even the wise cannot see him—and the Lord immediately appears to confront Job. The last two verses are an ironic transition to the next development.

Now that the speeches of Elihu have ended, the reader should take his measure. First, his very appearance is mysterious, since he is not mentioned elsewhere in the book, and he is the only Israelite among the group. While his adversarial position is understandable, he calls Job by name several times in a somewhat familiar way— this the friends never do. His comments betray a careful and detailed knowledge of some of Job's statements, even quoting them, as we have seen. However he is opposed not only to Job but to the three friends as well, as the introduction in 32:1–5 indicates. At the same time, he never makes clear exactly where the friends have failed, so preoccupied is he with his own "arguments." Considerations such as these have persuaded many that chapters 32–37 are a later addition to the book. Does he add anything to the points scored by the three friends? He insists more than they do that God does speak to human beings, but he shares their basic contention that suffering points to sin, and this is true in Job's case. Hence Job's defiance of God is totally out of order. Even though he improves on Eliphaz' statement about the disciplinary aspect of suffering (5:17) and underlines its medicinal character, he still affirms the traditional view, since "conversion" from sin is necessary in order to be restored. Finally, his last speech seems to be in some way a preparation for the theophany in Job 38. To all this one may reply that these considerations, even taken in their cumulative effect, are hardly enough to eliminate him. Any interpretation of the *book* cannot simply dismiss Elihu as a wayward item. Even if he is a "stray," the final author/editor interpreted him as part of the book. Brevard Childs has characterized Elihu's role thus: "The Elihu speeches function hermeneutically to shape the reader's hearing of the divine speeches. They shift the theological attention from Job's questions of justice to divine omnipotence and thus offer a substantive perspective on suffering, creation, and the nature of wisdom itself" (*Introduction to the Old Testament as Scripture* [Philadelphia: Fortress, 1979] 541).

Now the Lord will have the opportunity to speak, and this is "out of the storm." The Lord delivers two speeches, both meeting with short replies from Job. In view of Job's fears of how he might be received (e.g., 9:3–4, 11–16), the reply of the Lord is exceedingly moderate. One can surmise that the three friends, who are present (cf. 42:7) and doubtless would have expected God to destroy Job, are totally surprised.

7

God and Job
38:1–42:6

The Lord's First Speech (38:1–39:30)

IT DOES NOT TAKE LONG for the reader of the Lord's speeches to be baffled by them. God is full of surprises. He takes no cognizance of Job's predicament; it would have been so easy to go back and explain the test that was begun in chapters 1–2. And the reaction to the savage language of Job is surprisingly mild. He does not answer Job directly; he simply proposes a series of "unanswerable" questions, challenging Job's knowledge of various aspects of creation—unanswerable, but really loaded with meaning. Even the tone of the divine speeches is ambiguous. At first they may appear to be terribly sarcastic, almost as if the Lord lost a bit of his aplomb; this is true of 38:21. But for the rest, there is a more gentle mood of instruction, an air of "Don't you agree?" as the Lord sweeps through creation. One even gets the impression that he is rather proud of his various feats, that he is implicitly praising his own handiwork. Is the Lord sharing with Job his ongoing concerns about the world he has created? The poetic reach is magnificent, but what does Job learn about creation that he did not know before? Only in 40:8–14 is the basic issue touched on —and that is handled in a rather indirect manner. The subtlety of these final chapters makes it difficult to define precisely their function within the book.

38:1–3. Old Testament theophanies usually present the Lord as accompanied by earthly cataclysms (Exod 19:9–10; Jgs 5:4–5).

89

The Lord, who has not appeared or spoken since the prologue, begins with an aggressive reply to the challenges (e.g., 31:35–37) of Job, disregarding what has just been heard from Elihu. Job is "without knowledge" in speaking against the "plan" or "design" of God (v 2), which is left undefined. But he is to reply presumably on the basis of knowledge (!) to the Lord's questions. These turn out to be rhetorical, but they expose the "plan" that Job has darkened. Job had already admitted in 12:22 that God brings deep darkness to light, But there is no dialogue and no response from Job until 40:3–5, if that can be considered a response. Most of the time Job has expressed a demand for a meeting with God, especially in the context of a lawsuit and, often, with a fear that he' would be overwhelmed. But the yearning persisted (23:3–7). His final challenge (31:35–37) is now met with a gruff response, and he is invited to gird himself for the encounter. Curiously, the Lord opens with a question in the third person ("Who is this...?"). One wonders if he remembers Job's bold challenge in 13:22, "Call me and I will answer—or I will speak and you reply."

In this speech the Lord reels off an impressive array of his activities, creating the world, dealing with the Sea, providing light, covering the depths and the breadth of creation, providing snow and rain, concerns about the planets and the storms and various inhabitants of the animal world. There are many narratives elsewhere in the Bible that deal with creation, notably the somewhat dry, matter-of-fact account in Genesis l. But here the mood is important: this is a hymn of praise, ultimately, and it is the Lord who is praising himself, as he draws attention to his marvels! There is no talk about guilt or innocence. In fact the creation of man and woman is conspicuously absent. The Lord has much more to be concerned about.

38:4–7. A series of questions begins with Job's absence at the foundation of the earth. Where was he? He cannot be the primordial First Man, as Eliphaz taunted him (15:7–8). Neither is he Woman Wisdom, who was present with the Lord before and during creation (Prov 8:22–31). What is the purpose of these rhetorical questions?

They serve to mark the huge chasm between Job and the Lord. They are too outrageously impossible for Job to bother giving an answer. Of course, the reply to the questions is the Lord, and who cares where Job was? The portrayal of creation is that of a huge building; hence the reference to the architectural details, foundations, bases, and finally the cornerstone. An event of this importance would naturally be hailed, just as the buildings of earthlings are celebrated, with acclamation. The heavenly court ("morning stars, sons of Elohim") sings out with joyful praise of the new planet!

38:8–11. Water is ambivalent, absolutely necessary for life, yet threatening in terms of flood and mystery. Hence the Sea plays a great role in ancient mythology, and one of its functions is to personify chaos. Job has already spoken this way of the Sea in 3:8 (reading "Sea," not "day") and 7:12. Verse 10 indicates the divine containment of this unruly force, which is a frequent theme (e.g., Prov 8:22–31). What is unique here is the role of the Lord in the birthing details, vv 8–9. There is no battle with "Sea." It is a babe that issues from (whose?) womb, and tenderly wrapped in swaddling clothes—the very clouds themselves—by the Lord!

38:12–15. These lines draw an unusual picture: personified daylight takes up the earth by its "wings" or corners, and shakes it up. In an esthetic touch, the colors are portrayed as gradually appearing, with the earth standing out "like clay under seal." Is it significant that the wicked are mentioned here as being shaken *out* of the earth? Perhaps. If the earth is shaken, then somebody will have to fly out. But they are a minor detail in the picture, which follows a traditional line: darkness, not light, is the time for evildoing. The wicked are "rebels against the light," "friends of the terror of darkness" (Job 24:13–17). Darkness and night are the time for evil, or at least nonhuman activity, "when all the beasts of the forest stir" (Ps 104:20). They retire in the morning when human beings are up to be about their work. The good and the evil were frequently mentioned in the dialogue of Job and the friends, but this is the sole mention of the wicked in the divine speeches.

38:16–21. The furthest reaches of the universe are now touched upon. Has Job walked leisurely in the abyss *(tehom),* the original chaos (Gen 1:2) that God worked over at the beginning, or in Sheol within whose gates darkness is enclosed, and in which Job had the nerve to prefer to be (3:11–23)? Light and darkness are personified as having their respective "places," totally unknown to Job and also not mentioned in the rest of the Bible. After all, they were separated on the first day (Gen 1:3–4), and they had to be put in some place. Here Job receives the sharpest jab: You know, for you were born then (cf. also 15:7–9), when in fact only Woman Wisdom was present (Prov 8:22–31).

38:22–23. The Lord is pictured as having his implements for war on a cosmic scale, snow and hail, in storehouses. The warlike aspects are due to the havoc that these storms provided in Israel's memory (e.g., 1 Sam 7:10).

38:24–30. The mention of lightning (if the Hebrew term does not mean "wind") and thunder is to be expected in this litany of the cosmos. But what is striking is the emphatic repetition that the rain falls on "desert where there is no one," and the desolate waste becomes verdant. This question (25–27) raises more than the issue of place. What is the purpose of this prodigality? That implicit question is left unanswered. Verses 28–30 present an unusual picture: both male and female imagery is used to describe the fathering of rain and the birthing of dew, while ice issues— "from whose belly?" And water itself is "hidden" in ice, which is appropriately compared to a stone. Even "the face of the deep" is frozen over. These marvels are all held up to Job, but the tone is one of admiration and praise, such as is sounded in Pss 147:16–18 and Sir 43:13–22.

38:31–33. The mysteries of outer space are growing, even as modern discoveries reveal new stars. The "cords" to Pleiades and Orion refer to the control God exercises in leading them around. The identity of Mazzaroth (constellation?) and the "Bear" (Ursa?) is uncertain. The question about the "laws of the heavens" should not be embarrassing for Job, since it can be as well directed to modern astronomers.

38:34–38. The final mystery of the empyrean world is the clouds and rain (cf. already v 28); as always the issue is Job's impotence in controlling them. Although one can speak of the "Fertile Crescent," the relatively slight rainfall overall in Israel was often the occasion of drought and famine, and it is a modern dilemma as well. Outside of containing a challenge to Job's ability, the import of v 36 is not clear. "Mind" and "heart" have also been translated as animals, "ibis" and "cock." In vv 35–37 there is mention of divine channels for the rain; here rain is conceived as due to the divine tilting of water-skins in the sky, and thus the muddy plains of earth are formed.

38:39–41. The poet has finished the canvas of the cosmological mysteries, and attention is now given to the animal world, where divine providence extends from the least to the greatest, from ravens to lions, and even to the most intimate details of animal life. The contrast between the powerful, rapacious lion, so secure in finding its prey, and the predicament of the tiny raven is striking. It is all the more moving when their young are pictured as crying out to God in their hunger; cf. Pss 145:15–16; 147: 9.

39:1–4. Animal breeding was a serious concern in the ancient world, as Genesis 30 attests, but it is surprising to see the wild goats held up as an example here. Who supervises their periods for birth? The intricacies of gestation are known to the Lord, not to Job. Their life cycle is successful, but the young ones mature and then go off on their own.

39:5–8. The wild ass is associated with the wilderness, which is here depicted as a natural habitat that it prefers to the constraints of the "civilization" of the city, with its noise and shouting (v 7). No one controls the ass in the wasteland; there it must roam for food, but also the Lord has provided for water (Ps 104:11).

39:9–12. What a difference between the wild ox and its domesticated partner! Here is an animal that Job dare not and cannot tame. There is a kind of playful humor in the challenges that are recorded: can it be yoked for plowing or any other domestic need? Can it be trusted with anything?

39:13–18. The menagerie is all the more striking with the inclusion of the ostrich. (The text presents some difficulties and it is not found in the LXX; moreover it is a statement, not a question.) This animal is the epitome of cruelty, abandoning her eggs to dangerous chance and lacking in wisdom (this is God's doing!); a stupid animal, yet it laughs at those who would try to catch it.

39:19–25. The description of the war horse is one of the famous passages in this book. Its strength and readiness to enter into battle, its disregard for the weapons aimed at it, its excitement and eagerness at the sound of the trumpet are vivid traits of an impressive charger. Although it is not a wild, untamed, horse, there is something wild and indomitable about it in its zest for war and adventure; Job is confronted by another mystery.

39:26–30. The majestic flight of huge birds caught the imagination of the ancients: "the way of an eagle in the air" (Prov 30:19). The hawk and the eagle, from their craggy heights, can nevertheless spot a prey, even carrion, and provide for their young.

The first speech of the Lord is a veritable *tour de force*. The Lord is telling Job things that he knows, even if he can give no explanation. The Lord knows that Job knows the limitations in his range of knowledge, but it is all rather a diversion, not a condemnation that one might reasonably have expected from a deity who has been stirred by Job's language. The speech is so acutely irrelevant to Job's situation that it suggests we should approach it with imagination, not intellect. That is what G. K. Chesterton did, in the following passage:

> "The refusal of God to explain His design is itself a burning hint of His design. The riddles of God are more satisfying than the solutions of man... God says, in effect, that if there is one fine thing about the world, as far as men are concerned, it is that it cannot be explained. He insists on the inexplicableness of everything: 'Hath

the rain a father?.... Out of whose womb came the ice'? (38:28f.).
He goes farther, and insists on the positive and palpable unreason
of things: 'Hast thou sent the rain upon the desert where no man is,
and upon the wilderness wherein there is no man?' (38:26). God
will make man see things, if it is only against the black background
of nonentity. God will make Job see a startling universe if He can
only do it by making Job see an idiotic universe. To startle man
God becomes for an instant an atheist. He unrolls before Job a long
panorama of created things, the horse, the eagle, the raven, the wild
ass, the peacock, the ostrich, the crocodile. He so describes each of
them that it sounds like a monster walking in the sun. The whole is
a sort of psalm or rhapsody of the sense of wonder. The maker of
all things is astonished at the things He has himself made." (*G. K.
Chesterton: A Selection from his Non-Fictional Prose* [W. H.
Auden, ed.; London: Faber & Faber, 1970] 153–154).

Chesterton may have overstated the character of the divine
speeches, but he has also caught something of their mystery.

40:1–5. Job had asked for, even demanded, an arraignment in
a lawsuit with God (e.g., 31:35–37). The Lord now challenges
him to respond to the encounter. It is interesting that yhwh refers
to himself as Shaddai, as it were, in the third person. What has
Job to say for himself? Such is the sense of v 2. Job's reply is
probably not the type one would expect. He does not indicate
that he is bewildered by the Lord's address, nor does he raise
any of the questions that came so readily to his lips in the dialogue. His reaction is severely muted; literally he says: "I am
small." What does he mean? It is possible that he is being both
true, if he is humbly pondering the list of *mirabilia* in the divine
speech, but also perhaps evasive. Putting hand to mouth is an
accepted gesture of attention and reverence toward another; cf.,
Job 29:9. Does it mean here that he has said all that he deems
necessary, or perhaps that he needs more time to absorb this
overwhelming meeting? In any case, he declines to answer the
abrupt "invitation" to respond, issued in v 2. Instead, he chooses
silence (v 5).

40:5–14. Without further ado the Lord launches into another speech, introducing it with the same challenge as before (v 7=38:3). But now, and for the only time, the issue is stated sharply (v 8). This passage is not to be lost in view of the famous descriptions of Behemoth and Leviathan that follow. The Lord accuses Job in 40:8 of denying the divine right *(mishpat),* just as Job had made the same charge against God (27:2, 5). Now the shoe is on the other foot. He takes up again the interrogatory style in vv 8–9 and challenges Job, as it were, to play God! The supreme divine act is to consist in whether Job can defeat the proud and the wicked (vv 10–13). If Job can accomplish this, he will be acclaimed by the Lord: "Then I will praise you, for your right hand has won your victory" (v 14). The second part of that line is practically a repetition of the praise of the Lord in Ps 98:1, "His right hand has won him victory." What does this mean? Is the whole question at bottom an issue of power ("an arm like that of God," v 9) and not of justice? God *can* control, but he refuses to. I think that vv 9–14 drip with sarcasm and irony—the idea of Job trying to correct what God is doing, pronouncing judgment on the way he runs the universe! (After all, he "rains upon the just and the unjust" —Matt 5:45). God is not denying his own omnipotence, which is a presupposition of the book, but he is redefining the problem, as it were, shifting the focus from justice to the broader notion of sovereignty over the universe, and the designs he has for running it. He has no obligations; he is free to do as he pleases; he is affirming his independence of human judgment. The power to undo the proud is perhaps possible for a human to achieve, but God refuses to accept that criterion of justice. He is affirming what Job accused him of (e.g., 21:7–34)—letting off the proud and wicked unscathed. He will not accept human standards of judgment. Qoheleth insisted on this divine independence by underscoring the inability of human beings to understand what God is doing; cf. Eccl 3:11; 7:1; 8:17.

40:15–24. The transition to the description of the two great animals, Behemoth and Leviathan, is rather abrupt, but it strengthens the divine claim implied in vv 8–14. Behemoth is literally the plural of an ordinary Hebrew word for beast or animal, and here the plural is doubtless to emphasize the size and power of this particular monster. On the basis of the descriptions, Behemoth has been identified as a hippopotamus (as well as an elephant and buffalo), and Leviathan has been seen as a dragon or crocodile. However, when one recalls the mythical aura surrounding the powers of chaos, such as Rahab, or Yam (Sea), it seems preferable to recognize a mythical aspect to these animals. For the purposes of the Book of Job it is better to recognize the role, rather than the minute descriptions and identities of the animals. They are symbols of chaos. At the same time, they are a lesson for Job. If he is going to contend with the Lord, he should consider these choice creatures!

The origins of Behemoth are simple: made by the Lord, just as Job was, and even an eater of grass. But his strength is great (vv 16–17; the reference may be to his sexual prowess). There follows a series of quick images of his appearance, his appetite, and his watery habitat. The claim is made that he is "the first of God's works" (v 19), a masterpiece. Job is addressed indirectly by the question about the impossibility of capturing or controlling this beast. But direct sarcasm will surface in the description of the next animal.

40:25–41:26 = 41:1–34

Readers should note that the chapter and verse numbers of the Hebrew Masoretic text differ from many versions, which begin 41:1 with the first mention of Leviathan at 40:25 of the Hebrew. We will follow the Hebrew numbering and provide the other sequence in brackets.

Leviathan is described in many ways in the Bible. He is a seagoing creature that the Lord makes sport of (Ps 104:26), but in Ps 74:14, the many heads of this sea monster are smashed by the

Lord. Isaiah 27:1 describes him as a serpent ("fleeing"? and twist-
ing—a sea dragon), whom the Lord will put to the sword.

40:25–32 [41:1–8]. Leviathan is introduced in the sarcastic style
that marked the last word about Behemoth in 40:24. How could Job
ever contain him (vv 25-32 [41:1–8])! But the sarcasm is heavy:
what instrument would Job use? Would Leviathan treat Job gently
and even agree to be his slave? Is he like a bird to be played with?
Once you lay hand on him, you will never fight again.

41:1–26 [41:9–34]. The description of Leviathan goes into
great detail. After preliminary words about the danger he poses
(vv 1–4 [9–12], the text is uncertain), he is portrayed as a frightening figure, his body covered with an impenetrable armor of
interlocking scales, while his teeth inspire terror. Fiery flames,
those of a dragon, shoot forth from his eyes, nostrils, and mouth.
He is so firmly constructed that weapons aimed at him are useless: iron is straw, clubs are chaff, lances are greeted with laughter. When he rises up "the gods fear" (v 17 [25]). One can see him
moving through mud and water, leaving behind his imprint in the
mire and in the spumes of water that are stirred up. He has no
equal on earth, and is "king over all the proud." The speech of the
Lord ends suddenly, but the point is clear: Job and anyone else,
except the Lord, is helpless before the monsters of chaos.

At the beginning of the theophany (38:1), the reader's attention
was called to the unusual character of the Lord's response to Job.
Those considerations bear repetition, because the Lord's speeches
are not a response, or "answer" to Job's situation. Yet, in another
sense, they are, and every reader has to determine just how they are.

8

The Epilogue
42:7–17

Job's Final Words

THIS SECTION IS SO IMPORTANT that it is wise to set it apart,
although it logically belongs to the Lord's speeches, which
include Job's first response (40:1–5). There are textual
doubts concerning the beginning of 42:3 and 4, and some versions
omit 3a (=38:2a) and 4b (=38:3b), while others introduce phrases
like "you said" to indicate that Job is quoting. In vv 2–3 Job clearly
yields to the Lord and acknowledges the divine plans and power;
cf. 38:2; 40:8. In response to 38:2 he admits that he spoke about
things of which he was basically ignorant. Verse 4 reflects 38:3b,
God's command that Job listen and respond. The crowning verse is
v 5: "I had heard of you with the hearing of the ears, but now my
eye has seen you." This has been interpreted in two ways. There is
a contrast between "hearing" and "seeing." All the teaching gives
way before this direct encounter with the Lord. *Seeing* God, such
as the hope that Job had entertained in the vision of his *go'el,* or
Vindicator, in 19:25–27, is what changes Job. But perhaps no contrast is intended. Then 5b intensifies what Job has "heard" (the
divine speeches?) according to 5a. In either case, Job has been
changed by a more intimate experience of God, which the theophany conveyed. His previous contact with God was all hearsay. He
has experienced a profound transformation in light of which issues
of guilt, justice and injustice, charges and countercharges, have

vanished. Such is the meaning of v 5. It is v 6 that is puzzling, because it cannot be translated with certainty, due to the obscurity of the Hebrew text. The common interpretation is that Job recants (what he has said, or possibly, that he despises himself), and he "repents" on dust and ashes. The problem is to square this with 42:7, in which the Lord says that Job spoke rightly about him, in contrast to the three friends who did not. The issue in v 6 is: What is Job recanting and repenting of? These words have been interpreted to mean that Job is confessing to an excess in his language about God, and he is now sorry for this. But such an inference is gratuitous and can hardly be inferred from 38:2. The text says nothing about "excess." Second, it is claimed that Job performs some penitential rite, repenting on dust and ashes. Again, this is impossible in view of the praise of Job by God in v 7, and Job's intercession for the three friends. "Dust and ashes" can also stand for human mortality; it need not indicate repentance. Whatever be the translation of v 6, it cannot mean that Job goes back on the views expressed, however vigorously, in the debate, or repents for anything sinful. With all diffidence, I would suggest the following translation of 42:6: "Therefore I retract and change my mind, being but dust and ashes."

Epilogue (42:7–17)

There is a clear break at this point. The style changes, and the reader is back in the atmosphere of chapter 1. The movement of the narrative is quick: the friends, the relatives, the restoration of Job. Many commentators claim that the epilogue connects directly with chapters 1–2, and that the dialogue in the rest of the book is an insertion that conflicts with this "happy ending" story, which has Job rewarded for the resigned attitude he displayed in 1:21; 2:10. One can hardly question that the framework of the book is the prologue and epilogue (1:1–2:13 and 42:7–17), but there is no real profit in hypothesizing a conversation between the friends and Job different from what we have.

42:7–10. It may come as a surprise that the Lord is *angry* at Eliphaz and his companions. The reason is given succinctly: they did not speak "correctly" *(nekonah)* about him as Job did. How is this to be understood? The issue is not the anger but the "correct" speaking. The Lord has clearly given his approval to what Job has said. Is this possible after 38:2, 40:2, and the obviously tough language that Job has handed out against God? As we have indicated, some commentators find this dissonance insuperable and postulate that the "correct" words of Job refers back to his demeanor in chapters 1–2. Is there an alternative? The final editor either disregarded this dissonance, if he recognized it, or else he did recognize it but left it there anyway. He was doubtless aware of the complexity of the problem of the suffering of the just person, and could have deliberately left several voices sounding in the book. Even at cross purposes, these voices spoke to the problem with all the wisdom(s) available.

The words of the Lord to Eliphaz in v 7 give a clear verdict; he and his companions have succeeded only in arousing the divine anger. What irony here! It is "my servant" Job and not the defenders of God who has spoken rightly about the Lord. We have already pointed out the problem that this raises in the light of 38:2. The irony continues: they are to take the sacrificial animals to Job for a burnt offering; the Lord will hear his intercession on their behalf. Thus the word of Zophar about those who will seek Job's favor (11:19) turn out to be true, but not in the way that Zophar meant. It is another ironic trait that the three friends must have recourse to Job's intercession for them (vv 8–9). The final irony is that the author has used a very traditional story to explore a mystery in a very untraditional manner.

42:11–17. Many interpreters are put off by the fact that Job is given twice what he had before. Others have mistakenly considered the book as simply another happy ending story. But this fails to capture the spirit of the book. The restoration of Job is neither illogical

nor mistaken. It is not a "reward" for his conduct. It is as sudden
and unexplained as the catastrophes described in chapters 1 and 2.
Is Job to be left on the ashheap? Is it not also part of the divine freedom to grant surcease to those who suffer? As for the doubling of
Job's possessions, it has been noted that the doubling of former
possessions is specified as the award for damages in the case of
injustice (cf. Exod 22:4)—as though the Lord had been a thief!

The names of the beautiful daughters are exotic; respectively,
they mean "dove," "cinnamon," and "horn of eye-shadow" (the
Hebrew form is better: Keren-happuch). Moreover, they receive
an inheritance, along with their brothers, whose names are not
even mentioned, vv 14–15. Job's ending is described in typical
biblical terms—a long life and generations of grandchildren,
16–17.

Barbara Green has provided a perceptive interpretation of
Job's restoration (*New Blackfriars* 74/870; April 1993, 213–22,
esp. 219):

> The replacement of Job's wealth, blatantly and purposefully
> obscene, seems at first to undermine the whole point of the work.
> And in a way it does, but so that the work can start again. A hedge
> is back in place, with its dual power to protect and to restrict. Far
> from feeling relieved, angry or smug when Job is loaded up again,
> we ought to be apprehensive. What has happened once can happen
> again. Job, who of course represents here as always more than his
> individual self, is positioned for new adventures of one sort or
> another. We have returned to the equilibrium, the uneasy equilib-
> rium, of the prologue. And now we may be less sure what is good
> and what evil about it.

9

After-Thoughts

I T COULD PERHAPS BE EXPECTED that an attentive reading of the Book of Job would not leave much room for "after-thoughts." But that is not the way it is with a classic. The work has engendered many new insights in the course of transmission down the centuries. The history of the interpretation of Job, however briefly it is presented here, will be of some service to readers in helping them to understand their own reaction to the book.

A rather complete and far-reaching list of works has been provided by David Clines in the introduction to his commentary (*Job 1–20,* pp. lxiii–cxv), beginning with the patristic period and including also the Jewish tradition. The range is startling: not only literary works, but many of the arts, such as painting, music, dance, and film have felt the influence of this work. The history of the literary interpretation of Job would fill many books. It begins early on with the Greek translation of the work (the LXX). The Greek text is shorter than the Hebrew, and the translator(s) found it difficult to render. We are limiting the discussion to some of the classical literary works in both Christian and Jewish tradition, guided by the perceptive historical study of Susan E. Schreiner, *Where Shall Wisdom Be Found?* (Chicago University Press, 1994).

An early Targum (an Aramaic paraphrase, dating from about the beginning of the Christian era) of Job was found at Qumran, which is in general agreement with the Hebrew text that has been handed down to us. Early on, the biblical Job was interpreted in a pietistic way, as evidenced in the pseudepigraphic *Testament of Job* (cf J. Charlesworth, OPT I, 829–868; see also the brief interpretation of Aristeas the exegete, *OPT* II, 855–58). But in the later rabbinic tradition, Job the man becomes a problem not only because he contended with God but also because he was a Gentile. The whole question is also complicated by Jewish-Christian controversy. While Christians tended to exalt Job as a saintly pagan and an ideal for Christian patience (Origen, Jerome), the Jewish sages championed Abraham over him, and some also claimed, against the Christian view, that he was an Israelite.

The classic among the patristic writings is the *Moralia in Iob* of St. Gregory the Great (d. 604) [English translation: *Morals on the Book of Job* (Oxford: J. H. Parker, 1844–50)]. His 35 chapters had their origin in conferences to Benedictine monks and were dictated before the end of the sixth century. They became the source of moral and ascetical theology for centuries to come. He drew on many other biblical works (gospels, psalms) and portrayed Job as one who by his sufferings and endurance is the type of Christ and also the Church.

Gregory exemplifies for us several presuppositions or strategies for reading Job. An obvious one is his interpretation of the figure of the satan. Satan is the "devil" of New Testament thought. In chapter 1, Satan is among the "angels" because of his angelic nature, but he does not see God; he is only "before" the Lord. The question of the Lord, "Whence comest thou?" is equivalent to "I know you not," or divine condemnation. In fact, Gregory understands that the action is a contest between God (not Job) and the devil. Hence we cannot say that Job sinned in his strong speeches, or we would have to say that God lost the contest with the devil. No, the Lord knew Job would remain faithful, and that is why he called the devil's attention to Job in the first place. The crafty adversary claims that Job is let off easy, since God cares for him—but just let him be stripped of his possessions. Why does God allow this? "Ad augmentum muneris"—for the increase of Job's reward. It is clear that later theology has influenced Gregory in his broad interpretation of the scene. However, Gregory is acute in psychological observations. Job falls down at the news of the tragedy to his family and possessions—otherwise he would have been insensitive—and he also falls down to worship God, even though he is afflicted with great pain. At the end of his discussion, Gregory remarks that thus far he has followed the story line in the prologue and that should suffice. Then he deliberately turns to investigate "the mysteries of allegory." Here he interprets the devil's reply to the Lord's question concerning his whereabouts. He has been patrolling the earth, but only "to impress upon the hearts of the gentiles the footprints of his iniquity." Of course Job in his suffering becomes a type of Christ. It is informative for us to note how Gregory first interprets the story, and then deliberately announces his intention to seek the allegorical explanation. At least he knew exactly what he was doing. And he goes on to a moral consideration of the chapter. Thus, "the Lord gave and has taken away" should indicate in the reader a readiness to bear temporary loss as a sign that we have received our gifts graciously. The influence of Gregory's *Moralia* throughout the patristic and medieval period was simply immense.

However, the philosophical movements of the mediaeval period viewed the Book of Job in another light: the problem of providence. Two representatives are noteworthy: Moses Maimonides and Thomas Aquinas. The former discusses Job in *The Guide to the Perplexed* (University of Chicago Press, 1963) and the latter wrote a commentary *The Literal Exposition on Job* (Atlanta: Scholars Press, 1989). Both men were medieval Aristotelians, and this is evident in their interpretations, even though they differ. The issue for both is the divine providence. For Maimonides, Job comes off just, but unwise; for Aquinas, Job is wise, but not totally just. Both allow their respective traditions to impinge on interpretation, e.g., the immortality of the soul. For Maimonides, the work is a parable in which Job, a just man, seeks for wisdom through philosophy. For Aquinas, Job is wise, but ill-advised in the way in which he proceeds to teach the three friends.

Therefore the Christian student/teacher should learn from Job a practical lesson in communication. Job's extreme language is due to his extreme suffering, which is a characteristic of earthly life. But his belief in an immortal afterlife provided a solution to the harshness of living in this world.

In the Reformation period the work of Calvin is outstanding. His sermons on Job are reminiscent of the four sermons of Saint Ambrose. But there is no evidence that he had read the work of Ambrose, "On the Prayer of Job and David" (*De Interpellatione Iob et David* in CSEL 32/2; English translation in The Fathers of the Church series, volume 65; Washington: Catholic University Press, 1971, pp. 320–420). Ambrose and Calvin go their own way, but both explored in the laments of David and complaints of Job the common theme of suffering. Ambrose places the confession of Ps 73 with Job; they show the Christian how to suffer: "strength is made perfect in weakness" (2 Cor 12:9). Second, suffering leads one to see that true life is not to be had in the present. Suffering shakes one out of what Gregory the Great called the "fatal tranquillity" and leads to a higher view of God's ways. With Thomas Aquinas, Calvin thought that Job believed in an afterlife. For Thomas, this removed the terrible dilemma of trying to acknowledge and recognize the justice of God in this life. But Calvin struggles with the incomprehensibility of God's plan. Suffering creates problems about providence. Why is God now visible, now hidden; now clear and now dark? He prefers the psalms, and so David (and his humility) above the stark complaints and accusations of Job, which reek of self-justification. But Calvin cannot stop there. He recognizes that Job's suffering is inexplicable, that God remains hidden. One must trust that the God who controls nature will eventually straighten everything out. Until then, suffering is linked with the inscrutability of providence, the divine hiddenness. One receives some revelation of God in the realm of creation—enough to believe in the divine goodness and wisdom.

In recent times, two studies of the book of Job have received wide attention, those by G. Gutiérrez and R. Girard. The particular perspective of Gutiérrez is obvious from the Spanish title, which says literally, "To speak of God from the point of view of the suffering of the innocent." W. Vogels (*Job. L'homme qui a bien parlé de Dieu,* pp. 9–10) had already explored the topic of speaking of God in suffering, taking his cue from Job 42:7, in which the Lord asserts that Job has spoken correctly about him. When the issue is examined by a Latin American, it becomes a central question. Job is seen as one who suffers with the afflicted poor people. Gutiérrez attempts to show that there is a growing awareness in Job of his solidarity with the poor, and also God's preferential option for the poor. However, these are not the concerns of the biblical work. When Job speaks of the poor, it is in the context of refuting the theory of the friends, for whom the suffering of the poor is an anomaly: it is a temporary trial, or it may be deserved on account of sin, but can be eliminated by conversion. Job cries out brutally that God laughs at the calamity of the innocent (9:23). He is not unsympathetic to the fate of the poor, but their fate only compounds the larger problem of divine governance. The book does not argue there should be justice for all, although that would be a boon, but asks rather, why is God acting this way with Job? If one can in the end speak of the transformation of Job, it is not a transformation in which he goes out to a crusade for the poor, but is humbled before mystery.

In *Job. The Victim of His People* (Stanford: Stanford University Press, 1987) René Girard interprets Job as the scapegoat of his community. The driving idea behind the interpretation is that the innocent one becomes the focus of the hatred of others. Girard imposes a grid on the book—a psychological and anthropological theory of scapegoat: Violence among humans originates in a desire of imitating the other—hence rivalry arises and the model becomes the victim. If the imitation were ever acted out there would be social chaos, but this is avoided by the sacrifice of the rival, who becomes a kind of scapegoat. This approach raises two questions: Is it a valid insight into human behavior? And, does it really apply to the biblical Job? Girard does away with the narrative framework of the book and the speeches of the Lord; he

works only with the dialogues (*Job,* pp. 142–145). Thus far his
views have not attracted a significant following.

Countless other works bearing the imprint of the biblical book
could be mentioned. In the English speaking world, the play by
Archibald MacLeish was given more attention than it deserved. His
J.B. is not faithful to the biblical text. More sharp and pertinent, and
much less the size, is the long poem of Robert Frost, "The Masque
of Reason," in which God, Job and his wife, and Satan appear in a
dialogue. At the very beginning of the work God applauds Job for
having freed him to be God and to not have to reward good and
punish evil—in other words, the connection between justice and
reality can be broken; virtue may not bring the success it is supposed to bring, nor wickedness the required punishment.

Job—A Summary

After a "Short Reading," does it make sense to attempt a summary of the main point(s) of the Book of Job? Perhaps the following summary can be of some help in forming a general and
satisfying interpretation. Complete agreement is not to be
expected, because no matter how "objective" one strives to be,
there are certain presuppositions (even if unspoken, of which one
is not fully aware), that not all share, and which tilt the understanding of a passage or a chapter in another direction. Let the
reader weigh the following conclusions:

1. There is no *one* point of view concerning divine retribution
advocated in the book. Several important considerations about
human suffering and divine reaction are presented. Thus, it is not
adequate to claim that the traditional opinion concerning the prosperity of the just and the suffering of the wicked has been obliter-
ated. It has been shown as not valid in the case of Job and, by
implication, in many other cases. But it has been enunciated and
even defended with the best arguments available to the author at
the time. The author/editor has tried to be even-handed, while at

the same time upholding Job's arguments against those of the three friends. For him it was not a case of either/or; the mystery of divine governance remains. He knew no other way of dealing with the problem than by presenting conflicting viewpoints. There is a distant similarity to the book of Ecclesiastes. Basically the message of Qoheleth was "vanity," or the absurdity of what goes on in this world. At the same time, he offered resigned conclusions about snatching whatever "joy" may come your way (Eccl 2:24–26; 3:12,22; 5:17–18; 8:15; 9:7–9; 11:7–12).

2. From the point of view of theology, what is one to make of the conversation between *yhwh* and the satan in chapters 1–2? One may grant that there are certain liberties taken in this encounter, such as their apparently casual conversation about the loyalty of human beings. This seems to be the author's way of opening up the matter at issue. One may compare with it the importance of the conversation of the Lord with the man and the woman in Genesis 2–3. In a way, that conversation set the stage for the entire Bible. Similarly, chapters 1–2 set the stage for the dialogue between Job and his friends. At the same time, this scene raises an important theological issue in 1:9: Is a disinterested piety, a selfless love of God, possible? "Disinterested piety" is a terribly abstract way of putting the question so cleverly devised by the satan, "Is it for nothing that Job is God-fearing?" Even if doubt is cast on the credibility of Job's replies in 1:21 and 2:10, they are recorded there and represent a possible heroic stage of selfless love of God, and this question remains as a challenge for every human being.

3. The import of the dialogue between Job and the friends is multivalent. First, it is obvious that the basic theology of the friends is pointed in the wrong direction. While they say many things that in a given context might be respectable, and even agreeable to an Israelite reader, it is clear that overall their words are inadequate to the situation of Job. The author has captured the exaggeration, rigidity, and insensitivity that mark their discussions about divine retribution—without, however, ridiculing them; their theological judgment is untenable in the context. Second, Job is the mouthpiece of the

author in the attempt to find a new area of discourse. He is not above exaggerating Job's statements; that adds verisimilitude and reality to the dialogue. He is not concerned with justifying Job's utterances, however outrageous they are at times, any more than he is concerned with condemning all the words of the friends. An important emphasis is the unrestrained speech of Job. This is deliberate; it is true to life, as several psalms bear witness. And it prompts questions for us all: Is this not a legitimate way to speak of/to God in suffering? To what extent do faith and despair co-exist in one who suffers?

4. The function of chapter 28 is puzzling. First of all, the speaker is not clearly identified. While interpreters generally attribute it to Job, this is not necessary, as was pointed out above in the commentary. There is no identifying tag, nor does it have continuity with the previous chapter. It is not easy to see the connection of the 27 verses with v 28. But to call this chapter an "interlude" is a dodge. The reader must face the fact that the chapter is present where it is, and ask the question if it can be understood. As indicated above, it seems to be another attempt to deal with the problem created by the wisdom doctrine and recognized as one solution: We do not know the answer because we cannot find this hidden wisdom apart from fear of God. And even then, the fear of God (28:28; cf. 1:1, 8) guarantees nothing; one is left with the mystery of God. Chapter 28 is not an adequate statement for the problem posed by Job's suffering, but it is a consideration that has been placed within the book itself.

5. Elihu. The commentary has already indicated the doubts that have been raised about the pertinence of Elihu as a character, and also the significance of his speeches. At the most, he provides a fuller development of the medicinal character of suffering. His style does not appear to be as rigid as that of the three friends, but basically his theological position is the same as theirs. He leaves no room for Job's integrity. His description of the marvels of God in his final speech is well done, but it is difficult to be enthusiastic about his role. His intervention fails to give movement to the book. The chapters devoted to him could have been dropped with-

out any great loss, despite the fact that the author/editor understood him as "in place."

6. The speeches of the Lord have been scored as irrelevant by many readers. Is this an exaggerated judgment? If one allows that suffering is mystery, the speeches can be seen to have an effect that is not "explanatory," but challenging. Like Job, human beings are challenged concerning their own ignorance and their impotence. As "puzzling" as the response of the Lord is, it remains brilliant poetry and verges on the mystery that is intrinsic to the problem the author meant to explore. Why did the Lord not say, as Robert Frost has him say, that he had a deal going with the satan, but he knew that he could count on Job? That question is not worthy of an answer, or of the Book of Job itself. Probably the real justification for the Lord's speeches is simply the reaction of Job, whose intriguing terseness is worthy of the speeches of the Lord.

7. Job's reaction. Despite the uncertainty of the translation of 42:6, the words of Job in 42:2 and especially 42:5 suffice to convey a significant change in character. The fact that questions can still be raised, at least by modern commentators, about Job's "conversion" is a sign that the author had no easy answers to the fundamental question of suffering; he does not close the door on the mystery.

8. The epilogue especially has been questioned on several fronts: How is the verdict about the "correct" speech of Job (42:7) to be reconciled with his violent language in the dialogues? Does not his restoration nullify the drama of the work? It is shortsighted to object to Job's restoration for two reasons: God does act in surprising ways, even "rewarding" his servants; that is part of the mystery. Second, there would be a distinct feeling of an unfinished work if Job were simply to be left on the ashheap. But the tension between the correct speech about God and Job's previous language remains; this is concretized by the Lord's questions in 38:2; 40:2, and his statement in 42:7. The problem arises with Job as well. How does his admission in 42:3 gibe with the Lord's approval in 42:7? Is this dissonance theologically and psychologically tenable? The author/editor was not

deterred by it and allowed the dissonance to stay, or perhaps better, resolved it by understanding 42:7 as a global statement.

C. Newsom has described the Book of Job as resembling "the
Gestalt drawing that can be seen in two irreconcilable ways, as a
duck or a rabbit, a goblet or facing profiles" (*Biblical Interpretation*
1/2 [1993] 137). This pictorial metaphor catches the ambiguities one
finds in the book. But perhaps the final word on this summary
should be taken from St. Augustine in his *Confessions,* XII, 30–32
(*The Confessions of St. Augustine* [Translated by F. J. Sheed; New
York: Sheed & Ward,1954] 315–16). He is commenting on the
opening verses of the Bible, Gen 1:1–2, but his views are applicable
to the reader of Job. In the following quotation he assumes that
Moses is the author of Genesis: "Thus when one man says to me:
'Moses meant what I think,' and another 'Not at all, he meant what I
think,' it seems to me the truly religious thing to say: Why should he
not have meant both, if both are true; and if in the same words some
should see a third and a fourth and any number of true meanings,
why should we not believe that Moses saw them all, since by him
the one God tempered Sacred Scripture to the minds of many who
should see truths in it yet not all the same truths…. When he
[Moses] was writing these words he wholly saw and realized whatever truth we have been able to find in them—and much beside that
we have not been able to find, or have not yet been able to find,
though it is there in them to be found." If one allows for almost two
millennia in the development of hermeneutics, the reader may find
Augustine very modern. His approach resembles the current reader-
response theory, but in the search for truth; he knows who the true
"author" is: "God tempered Sacred Scripture."

The Text of Job

The problem is the ending of the dialogues, chapters 22–31.
This short treatment aims to point out the alleged inconcinnities
in the final "cycle" of speeches between Job and his friends, so

that the reader has a broader base of knowledge on which to judge the rearrangements that are so frequently found in commentaries. Although the final monologue of Job, chapters 29–31, does not really figure in this problem, they are indicated here more as a cutoff point, The obvious difficulties occur in chapters 25–27, and they can be succinctly described:

1. The disappearance of Zophar, who has appeared in regular turn in the earlier chapters. Joined with this fact is the extreme brevity of Bildad's speech, only six lines, 25:1–6.

2. The variation represented by the introductory verse, or heading. The usual formula is "X said" (literally, X answered and said). But 27:1 reads: "Job again took up his discourse and said." This singular introduction would suggest that there had been an interruption, although chapter 26 is given to Job and is introduced by "Job answered and said" (26:1).

3. The absence of any introduction to chapter 28. Normally, this would indicate a continuation of the previously mentioned speaker, who in this case is Job. But it is difficult to associate the content of chapter 28 with the character of Job's speeches. More-over, chapter 29:1 opens the same way as 27:1, "Job again took up his discourse and said." Such an introduction would also suggest that chapter 28 is interruptive—in this case, interrupting Job's speech to Bildad in chapter 27, which is not without its own prob-lems. (How do 27:13–23 fit in with Job's point of view?) Hence some commentators speak of chapter 28 as an "interlude," per-haps written by the author, or as a later insertion.

4. Finally, there are certain passages that are difficult to square with Job's statements, because they seem to be in harmony with the views of the friends. Therefore they are considered to be the "missing" verses claimed for Bildad and Zophar. Among the passages in question are 24:18–24; 26:5–14; 27:13–23.

There is no question that these are solid reasons for question-ing the sequence of chapters and verses at this point. But the fol-lowing contrary considerations deserve to be heard:

1. The history of the transmission of the book gives no evidence that a different sequence of chapters and verses ever existed. This evidence goes back far—to the time that the Targum of Job (found at Qumran and dated around the first century B.C.) was written, and even before that, to a period when the Greek translation (LXX or Septuagint) was made. Hence one is reduced to unprovable assertions: the text was changed by accident or deliberately, for whatever reasons.

2. The fact is that no reconstruction of the "original" sequence has been able to find a consensus among scholars.

3. Are the alleged dislocations in the text so serious that they call for reconstruction? For example, is the disappearance of Zophar a problem? Could it not be that the author/editor intended this as a sign that the debate had come to an end, or at least an impasse, and that Job was not to be bested? Also, could one explain the few verses attributed to Bildad as a similar sign?

4. Is it possible to understand the "questionable" passages attributed to Job as fitting into his overall position vis-a-vis the friends, that he is really describing their lot—they are the "wicked"?

These considerations do not answer all the difficulties, but they are the reason why this commentary chose to follow the sequence of the Hebrew text, with only brief indications of the problematic passages, and their possible meanings.

10

Does the Book of Job Have a Theology?

N O MATTER HOW ONE ATTEMPTS to compose a "theology" of the Bible, or even of one biblical book, one's personal evaluation and organization of the biblical data produce an inevitable "slanting" of the material. One makes value judgments as to the centrality and importance of certain ideas, and hence the "theology" is somewhat subjective. Allowing for this, should more be said about theological themes that are present, some new and some old? There is not much profit in repeating theological ideas that are found clearly expressed elsewhere. But there are some new insights in Job, or at least a significant reuse of old insights, that deserve further consideration. We have already indicated something of the afterlife of the book, the way it has been interpreted in the past. We have also attempted a summary of answers to the obvious question: what is this book all about? Perhaps the real question is the one pointed out in the Introduction: what does the book do to you if you read it? Even if one could capture them all, the answers to that question would be wide-ranging. Perhaps it is more helpful to single out issues immediately prompted by the book itself. Commentators are usually compelled to deal with such questions as theodicy and the justice of God, the suffering of the just person, guilt and deliverance, retribution, and so forth. One could expand this list and discover that they cross one another in this multilayered book. There is not always one answer to even our "obvious" question. Nor is it desirable to prioritize a list of primary topics. I merely aim to make explicit some of the theological issues that might either be taken for granted or get lost in the back and forth of the dialogue.

The reader should not be deceived by the term "theology," as though one might carry away one or more great truths of the Bible. There are so many different answers to any one theological issue in the Bible that the reader of one book, namely Job, might be tempted to make this one book the pivot of theological thought in the Old Testament. Even more important than this is the distinction between what is true and enduring from what is merely culturally conditioned, a mere world view, in biblical thought.

1. God. Of course, "God" is inevitable in a portrayal of biblical theology. It is difficult to write intelligently about God, even if so many have attempted to do so. We are encroaching on mystery, and can say more about what God is not rather than what God is. Yet the portrayal of God in this book calls for some discussion. Jack Miles entitled his Pulitzer Prize winning best-seller, *God A Biography* (New York: Random House/Vintage, 1996). This portrayal was a "literary" biography of God narrating the characteristics of the deity as they emerged across the canon of the Hebrew Bible. The chapter on Job, entitled, "Fiend " (certainly not Friend!), is a challenging discussion, but there are several questionable assumptions by the author. One of these is the simple identification of the satan with the devil—the Lord is called "the devil's gaming partner." The satan of the Old Testament is *not* the *diabolos* or devil of the New Testament. There is also a hypothetical rendering of a key text, Job 42:6, which we have discussed above in the commentary.

However, it may be asked if the average reader of the Book of Job is not deeply disturbed by a common interpretation, namely, the light and dark sides of the divinity, the divine and the demonic. The question was raised explicitly in the commentary on Job 1–2: what kind of a God is this *yhwh?* It is not fair to dismiss the question with a distinction between an ontology (with which these chapters are not concerned) and anthropomorphism (which does characterize the chapters). Anthropomorphic language, however inadequate it may be, is inescapable when speaking of divinity. The fact remains that the Israelite could and did conceive of the Lord as portrayed in the opening chapters. This is not something really new. There are many similar anthropomorphic descriptions throughout the Bible. Sometimes they are taken for granted, unless they are carefully read and questioned. One of the most picturesque and intriguing is the Lord's dinner with Abraham in Genesis 18. In point of fact, the Lord did not have dinner with Abraham or catch Sarah denying that she had laughed at the announcement of a birth within the year. The anthropomorphic character of that scene stands out more clearly than the scenario in Job 1–2. In both cases the versatility of the reader's interpretation is tested; the reader is dealing with an imaginative scene. This is not to deny the pertinence of the questions or objections that a modern reader can put forward. But it is a caution against drawing premature conclusions, since we so easily pass judgment, assuming our point of view is the correct one. To return to Job 1–2, it is to be admitted that the Israelite has no difficulty with the manner in which the Lord is portrayed in the book's opening chapters. But to speak of the combination of the divine and the demonic in God is really a projection of the human mind; Israel and ourselves remain ignorant of such an inner aspect of the divine life.

Although the phrase, *Deus absconditus,* or "hidden God," is not found in Job, it can easily be applied, and it has been popular among theologians, especially since Martin Luther. The phrase itself is biblical: "Truly with you God is hidden, the God of Israel, the savior!" These words are the acclamation of the gentiles in Is 45:15, acknowledging *yhwh,* unknown to anyone else but Israel, who is the savior of his people. So the phrase does not indicate in the first instance the mysterious and perplexing presence/absence of God. But the Latin phrase, which comes from the Vulgate rendering of Is 45:15, was picked up by many theologians who recognized how neatly it described an aspect of the Lord. The idea is genuinely biblical. God is frequently described as "hiding his face," as in Ps 104:29, with fatal consequences for his creatures. The contrary aspect is God letting his face shine on his creatures with beneficent effect, as in the priestly blessing, Num 6:25. In Job and also in the psalms, it usually occurs in a threatening or doleful context of displeasure. Job complains in one moment that God is hiding his face, and treating him as an enemy, 13:24, and in another, that God is "watching" him intently to catch any wrongdoing, 10:14. In the famous chapter 23 there is no "hiding" of the face, but the absence of God is underlined:

> But if I go east, he is not there;
>   or west, I cannot perceive him;
> Where the north enfolds him, I behold him not;
>   by the south he is veiled, and I see him not. (23:8–9)

But even in this lamentable state, Job must confess that the presence of God terrifies him, 23:15. Such a psychological condition aptly conveys the paradoxical nature of the (perhaps "elusive"?) presence and absence of God. David Tracy has articulated this aspect for the present day: "We must be willing, religiously and theologically, to face the dialectic of the revelation of God's radical hiddenness as we—and the Bible—experience that hiddenness in life, just as many theologians are now more willing to face our profound ignorance of God by rethinking the often marginalized apophatic mystical traditions of Christian thought, especially Meister Eckhart" ("The Hiddenness of God," *Cross Currents,* Spring 1996, 3–16, esp. 13).

Intrinsic to the divine hiddenness is divine freedom. Again the paradox: the more we "see" God, the more we tend to tame the divinity. This is not difficult to do; the Bible provides us with a slew of insights into the merciful and caring aspects of God, while we practically black out the more disturbing features of the divinity, till we have formed the notion of God that we can live with.

This is why the book of Job is so important. It upholds divine freedom, the right of God to be God. Such is an insight expressed by Robert Frost in his poem, "The Masque of Reason." The Lord appears to Job and his wife, living on an island. She recognizes him at once as the Lord because, she says, she would know him anywhere from Blake's pictures! The Lord puts off Job's questions about heaven to thank him for the way he helped him—the "great demonstration" they put on. It was a question of freedom. The human race was holding him to a neat law: God *had* to reward and punish evil. But Job changed all that; he set God free to reign, set God free to be God.

    2. Creation. Because creation is not a prominent theme in the New Testament (but cf. Col 1:15–16), it is usually understood in terms of the opening pages of the Bible. Genesis 1 is the majestic Priestly tradition of creation in a seven-day framework. The Israelite power of imagination was also able to cast this sober fact in poetic writings reflecting the various creation myths of its neighbors, the *Enuma Elish* in Mesopotamia; the Baal epic in Ugarit. Although less well known, the description of the creative acts of God in Job 38–40 are just as impressive. The rhetorical questions have the purpose of moving Job to another point of view. But the list of items is what we are interested in. They display a remarkable imagination and insights into various aspects of the divine creativity, from the foundations of the earth to the clouds and rains from heaven, 38:4–38. This is followed by specific examples from the animal kingdom (38:39–39:40, lion to eagle), culminating with Behemoth and Leviathan. Perhaps the most tantalizing omission is the creation of humans, a theme that appears so often throughout the Bible, explicitly and implicitly. Other biblical references often stress the ease with which the Lord creates; in Job it is the marvelous variety that is pointed out —a variety that challenges the reader to ponder what the providence of God truly means.

3. World-View. By this I mean an understanding of reality that is culturally conditioned and tangential to the biblical message, such as, the three storey conception of reality: heaven, earth and nether world. This is a delicate distinction, held by many who would interpret the creation and other narratives in a fundamentalist manner. I am not in favor of simply discarding an antiquated world-view; I want simply to recognize it for what it is. It can be challenging and provocative of other insights, but it is not of itself a theological datum. The Book of Job illustrates two important examples, the heavenly court and Sheol.

A. *The Heavenly Court.* This is a group whom the Lord includes in his entourage (e.g., Gen 1:26; Is 6:2–3, 8, and often). In post-biblical thought they have been assimilated into an artistic existence as "angels" and have correspondingly received a special kind of existence. But the biblical notion is that they are demoted deities. Such seems to be a correct inference from Ps 82 and other passages, e.g., Deut 32:8–9. They serve as the "inner circle" of the divinity, with whom God takes counsel (e.g., "who will go for us" in Is 6:8). They are called upon in Ps 29 to glorify the Lord; they also serve as his messengers. Hence they are named "angels," a term derived from the Greek word for messenger. It is they, and not human beings, who are called sons of God in the Old Testament. Their role in the Book of Job is to provide a *mise-en-scène,* with one of them playing the role of adversary or satan, who is an "angel," sent out to patrol the earth. The ambivalence of this figure was noted above in the commentary and needs only to be recalled here. His concern is that the Lord not be duped by the apparent integrity of Job. He is willing—and this doubtless is for the sake of the story that the author wishes to evolve—to put his own judgment up against that of *yhwh.* The theological issue is manifold. First, how much reality did the writer invest in these scenes? That is the same question about factuality that was raised above in the discussion concerning Abraham and the three visitors in Genesis 18. Second, one should rather ponder the function of the adversary, as well as the functions of all the members of the heavenly court throughout the Bible. It is in their function that their importance lies.

B. *Sheol.* The same kind of reasoning applies to Sheol or the nether world. Is it a belief? Are the descriptions of Sheol imaginative flights, such as in Job 3, which speaks of Sheol and its denizens: kings, counselors, princes—all the great people? And the little people—stillborn, wicked, weary prisoners—dwell there, the slave along with the taskmaster. Where do mortals go when they die (Job 14:10)? They sleep, not to awaken, in darkness. How is one to understand all this? The dead, or "shades" as they were called, had to be somewhere; so Sheol is postulated. It seems to be inherited from surrounding cultures, such as Mesopotamia, where it is also described as the place of no return. But of course no one had any first-hand knowledge of it, since no one had ever returned from there. It is not a place of judgment; it exists for everyone, the good and the bad. It is simply the other side of death. Indeed Death and Sheol are word pairs occurring very often parallel with each other, as in Cant 8:6. But nothing is really known about the other side, and hence free rein can be given to the imaginative descriptions of it. It is said that one is in Sheol, but the "one" is never defined except as an individual person who has died or will die. There is no speculation as to "what" is there, e.g., the "soul." No answer is given until the very end of the Old Testament period, e.g., Dan 12:1–3; Wis 1:15. I am describing world-view, not theology. Yet there is a kind of theological function to Sheol. It is not beyond God's reach or power, but whoever is there is described as having no *loving* contact with the Lord. Hence the psalmist prays to stay alive in order to praise God, e.g., Ps 6:5–6 and often. It is also used in a metaphorical or dynamic sense to describe troubles in *this* life, the kind of non-life or afflictions with which mortals are so often burdened. In that case, one is "in" Sheol even while living; hence the psalmist can proclaim, "*You* have brought me up from Sheol!" in order to express deliverance from some affliction (Ps 30:3–4). Let it not be thought this world-view is simply to be dismissed. It is to be pondered and evaluated in the light of Old Testament belief. Modern people who are over-eschatologized, who think of this life *only* in relation to an afterlife, may need to purify their faith. Too often one hears an astonished reaction to the biblical view: "How did these people believe in God?!" This is a foolish question, as if belief were dependent upon the existence of an afterlife. Faith means taking God on God's terms, whatever they are.

4.   Retribution. While this is not the main point of the Book of Job, it is a significant factor, and it catches the modern imagination: does God reward and also punish? There are many ramifications to that simple question. Perhaps the most important is the connection that was perceived to exist between sin and suffering. It was taken for granted that wrongdoing would be requited by some kind of evil, and that virtuous action would be rewarded by blessing. Thus the blessings are prosperity, long life, a progeny, and so on (cf. Job 29). The opposite can be illustrated by many of the speeches of the friends: the wicked person dies early, with an evil progeny, leaving behind no good name, and so forth. Ultimately, the justice of God is judged by these human standards. This view is governed by a limited perspective: requital had to take place in *this* life. But there is further exacerbation to the problem of retribution: its collective and individual aspects. The sense of collectivity is uppermost in the biblical world, contrary to the modern attitude. We are also aware of our collective identity —an association with our immediate and extended families, our religion and parish, our city and country— but we are very individualistic. Divine requital had an extended reach. The Lord is understood to be compassionate and gracious, "extending kindness to the thousandth generation, forgiving iniquity, transgression, and sin; yet he does not remit all punishment, but visits the iniquity of parents upon children and children's children, upon the third and fourth generation" (Exod 34:7). The reach of corporate togetherness is exemplified in the intriguing conversation between the Lord and Abraham as they walk towards Sodom. "Can I hide from Abraham what I am about to do?" the Lord says (Gen 18:17). He tells Abraham, who then challenges him: "Will you really sweep away the just with the wicked? Suppose there are fifty just people in the city...?" In the famous altercation Abraham narrows his request from fifty just people to ten, before the Lord escapes from him. It should be recalled also that in the case of the destruction to come upon Jerusalem, not even the presence of the triad, the just Noah, Daniel or Job himself, would suffice to preserve the city (Ezek 14:14).

The claim has been made that there was a mechanical connection between the deed and its consequence: a good act produces good results, and an evil act is rewarded with evil consequences. This point of view is graphically expressed in the proverb that one falls into the hole one has dug for another (Prov 26:27; Sir 27:26; Ps 7:15–16 and often). This mentality is not absent from much of the thinking of the three friends. However, it should not be absolutized, as if it expressed a sheer mechanical relationship, a kind of boomerang effect of an action. Even more often blessing or punishment is attributed to the direct intervention of the Lord.

The crux in the theory of reward and punishment is in the ease with which one reasons backward: suffering is a sign of wrongdoing on the part of the sufferer; prosperity is a sign of virtuous action. It is the fundamental mistake of the three friends in their argument, and it may be said to be a prime target of the author/editor of the book. Moreover, this mentality is not rare in the Old Testament. It is reflected in the great song of the suffering servant in Isaiah 53. The astonishment of those who behold the servant expresses that attitude; they had supposed that the servant was suffering for his own sins. But no! "He bore our infirmities and carried our diseases; but we accounted him stricken, struck down by God and afflicted. But he was wounded for our transgressions...." (53:4–5). This understanding is new and unique; suffering is seen to be redemptive for others.

The connection between sin and suffering appears in several psalms of lament. The lament is often a clean admission of sin, and thus it justifies the Lord's punishment, as in Ps 51:6. "Against you alone have I sinned and done evil in your sight; (I say this) so that

you are justified in your sentence and blameless in your judgment."
Here the confession is made to exonerate the Lord; the psalmist
admits sinfulness (v 5) and the ensuing punishment (v 10, the
crushing of the bones) as appropriate. But there are also laments
that are really complaints to the Lord for not intervening to deliver
the psalmist who is unjustly afflicted. Thus, Ps 26 claims innocence
(vv 4–8) and appeals to the Lord's justice (v 1). At bottom, this
reflects the dilemma that Job faced. Although innocent, he is suffering; why? It was a great scandal that the vaunted justice of the Lord
was not perceived as operative. Hence, Ps 37:1 (cf. Ps 73:1–3)
issues a warning: "Do not be provoked by evildoers; do not envy
those who do wrong." One must trust in the Lord to intervene. The
sharp division between the just and the wicked was laid out at the
very beginning of the psalter. Two ways confront a person. The
Lord watches over the one, while the other is the way of doom;
Ps 1:6. It is ironic that so many fail to recognize the ambiguities of
retribution, even though they are laid out in the Bible.

5. Spirituality. It was not a mistake on the part of James (Jas
5:11) to praise Job and hold him up as a model. It is just that he is a
model of steadfastness, endurance *(hypomonē)*, not of "patience,"
as that word is understood in modern parlance. Job, to use a slang
expression, "hung in there." And therewith are lessons in spirituality. We are using the term in a broad sense to designate a whole-
some relationship to God. While one can single out specific
aspects of spirituality, we will deal with only two here: Job's honesty with God and the role of testing in the spiritual life.

Job's honesty consists in his dogged determination to expose
himself to God rather than take refuge in the deceptive traditions
handed down by the three friends. Ultimately, theirs was a consoling doctrine, and it also had its truthful components. But these simply did not fit Job's situation. He could not deny his own experience
in order to satisfy orthodox theory, to "justify" God, as the friends
attempted to do. Job's integrity consists precisely in the courageous
duel with the friends, in which he is necessarily cast in the role of

blasphemer and reprobate, as the friends remind him. This is fierce honesty, which is given all the greater verisimilitude by the author/editor who gives Job the role of "wrecker." Gerhard von Rad wrote that Job's mistake was to claim that "God must." Thus, God "must" correct the mistake in afflicting Job in the first place. But what else must God "must?" There is no indication in the book that God must give him back what he has lost, must restore him to his former condition. Job never asks for that. The question is deeper, and in a sense, simpler than that. The question is: Why? Because Job's relationship to God has been shattered. What is the index of this relationship? Job's prosperity (cf. chapter 29)? No, there is no "index"; there is only a mysterious God who is pounding him. The Book of Job is concerned with relationship to God, not with the rise and fall of material possessions.

But do not Job's fluctuations between hope and despair ulti- mately designate him as a poor spiritual risk? Is not his extreme, even abusive, language a sign that this character was never intended as a biblical model? As for the fluctuations, there is no point in squaring the statements of faith against the statements of despair and expecting an answer. Psychological reality does not work that way. Moreover, we are dealing with a literary work. The author is seeking verisimilitude in the portrayal of an innocent person who is afflicted with suffering. What are they likely to say? The author inherited from the psalter a strong and lively tradition of remonstrance with God, but also a tradition of faith/trust in God, to inspire his portrayal. Significantly, both blasphemy and fidelity can be found. This trans- lates into a more correct evaluation of events from the point of view of moral theology. A "sin" of despair cannot easily be clocked, if at all. Those who suffer do not remain at one point; they are up and down, faithful and despairing together. And those who care for them must recognize this and refuse to clock them at any given point. Many raise a pastoral question: how can the Book of Job be used for the benefit of those who are suffering? There is no one answer. But the attempt should be made to utilize the work in some way—per- haps the reading of it, not the "preaching" of it, will succeed as an

opening move, while one leaves the rest to the grace of God. It may
be of some help to observe how little space is given to any description of Job's physical sickness. As a matter of fact we do not know
the exact nature of Job's physical affliction. The familiar "boils," or
"sores," or "inflammation" are attempts to render a difficult term in
2:7, but are described as covering his entire body, and the text says
he used sherds to scrape himself. Apart from 2:7–8, references to
physical suffering are rare. Indeed most of the time the affliction is
clothed in metaphors; a parade example would be Job's description
of the divine assault against him in 16:12–13: "I was at ease, and he
broke me in two; he seized me by the neck and dashed me to pieces;
he set me up as his target; his archers surround me. He slashes open
my kidneys and shows no mercy; he pours out my gall on the
ground" (NRSV). The description of troubles in the psalms is similar. In Ps 22, the language is so extravagant and the metaphors so frequent that one is at a loss to determine the suffering of the psalmist.
Thus there is mention of bulls, dogs. the sword, the mouth of the
lion, the horns of wild oxen; perhaps the references to the body in
v 15 are meant literally. This kind of language is not a disadvantage
to the modern reader. It is so highly metaphorical, that one can find it
suitable to apply to oneself.

The masters of the spiritual life leave room for divine testing.
This may be included under various terms, such as "the dark night
of the soul," or simply called suffering. The testing of Job is obvious from what we have written above. It is fruitful to align it with
another famous test in the Old Testament, that of Abraham in Genesis 22. Abraham's story is explicitly introduced as a "test" (22:1).
The narrative is a masterpiece in its succinctness, its directness.
Abraham is to sacrifice Isaac, "your only son, whom you love," and
sacrifice him as a burnt offering on Mt. Moriah (we can not locate
this mountain geographically). This stunning command is met with
simple and silent obedience as Abraham departs early the next
morning with son and servants. As he approaches the place, he sep-
arates the boy and himself from his two servants and goes up to
"worship" (literally, "prostrate oneself"). The journey proceeds in

the same laconic style, as Abraham places the wood on his son, while he carries the "fire" and knife—as if to keep the youngster out of harm's way. Astutely, Isaac calls his attention to the readiness for the sacrifice, but "where is the sheep?" Oh, God "will see to it" (or provide), is the answer (do not skip to v 14 for the answer that the Lord sees). When they arrive at the "place which the Lord had told him," Abraham goes into a series of actions quickly spelled out by seven verbs: building an altar, placing the wood, binding Isaac, and putting him on the altar over the wood. Then he picks up the knife to slay him. At this point one should stop and assess the meaning of the narrative, which is rightly termed in Jewish tradition "the binding of Isaac." The question that was raised in the first chapter of Job comes to mind: What kind of a God is this? Equivalently, what is God asking Abraham to do? The modern reader is shocked at the idea of child sacrifice, and sympathy for the father's grief comes readily to the fore. But that is to miss the point. In the ancient world child sacrifice was not the gruesome action we consider it to be. It was an act of religion, of worship; one offered the first fruits of the family. Hence an emotional identification with a suffering father is not truly relevant.

Then what is the issue here? For this we have to go back to a series of events that began to be related in Genesis 12. There Abraham was told by the Lord to leave his father's house for the land that he would show him. Abraham was to be given a country (somewhere!) and become a great nation, and in some way be a blessing to all the families of the earth (12:1–3). This grandiose design is simply and obediently carried out by Abraham. But the author puts it in context: Abraham was 75 years old when he left (v 4), and Sarah's sterility was noted in Gen 11:30. It is in this somewhat unfavorable situation that Abraham simply obeys. But the situation does not improve. Although God assures him more than once that he will have a child (Gen 12:7; 13:16), there is reason to wonder. Again with marvelous narrative simplicity, Abraham replies to God's renewed promise of a reward that he "shall die childless" (15:2). Would it not be better to designate his servant Eliezer as the heir? But no, the Lord shows Abraham the stars to count—such will be his *own* progeny. And there is the telling judgment: Abraham believed the Lord and it was reckoned to him as righteousness (15:6). As Sarah's sterility continues, she proposes that Abraham raise a family through Hagar, her Egyptian maid. So Ishmael is born of Hagar. Again the Lord appears to Abraham and reiterates the great promises—specifically Sarah is to have a child (17:16). At this Abraham fell down before him, laughed *(yishaq),* and to himself expressed doubts that a man 100 years old could expect to have a child from a woman aged 90. Let the child of promise be Ishmael! But again, no—it is specified that Sarah will a bear a son named Yishaq, that is, Isaac (the name means "he [God] laughs"). And the Lord affirms that the covenant with Abraham will be kept. In chapter 18 the Lord appears, one of "three men" to Abraham. (The presence of the three at the ensuing meal has been caught on the famous icon, *Trinita,* of the Russian painter, I. Rublev.) During the meal, the whereabouts of Sarah is raised. She is back in the tent, but as it turns out, eavesdropping sufficiently to hear the reiteration of that famous promise; this time next year….And Sarah laughed *(tishaq,* the feminine form of *yishaq)* at the idea of herself and her husband having a child at their advanced age. Obviously every time the future child is brought up, there is a play on his name; both Abraham and Sarah are laughing, or better, it is God who laughs! But now there is an ingenuous turn in the narrative. One of the guests, identified as the Lord, renouncing anonymity, catches Sarah out: Why did she laugh? There will be a son by next year! Then Sarah lies, denying that she laughed (for she was frightened), only to be told by the Lord: "You *did* laugh!"

The narrative is so charming that we almost forget the reason for bringing it up. The point was to illustrate the significance of the "binding" of Isaac. Now we can understand the magnitude of what God was asking Abraham to do. It was more than the sacrifice of a child. It was more than a case of obedience. Indeed, is there any word that can convey Abraham's openness to God? In effect, he had been told to cut off the only reasonable hope that remained for the fulfillment of the promise, the keeping of the covenant. Abraham was being asked to permit God to go back on his word, in effect to cancel the covenant that had finally displayed some shadow of fulfillment in the birth of Isaac. This is the incredible test. It should not be softened by the fact that God suspends it, and the ram caught in the thicket replaces Isaac—a special typological relationship is seen here by the author of the letter to the Hebrews (Heb 11:11–12, 17–19). It is doubtless the example of Christ that inspired New Testament writers to conceive of testing in such noble words as Rom 5:3–4; James 1:12.

The tale of Abraham and Isaac has stirred artists and thinkers down the ages. The most telling "continuation" of the narrative is that given by Søren Kierkegaard in his *Fear and Trembling.* He imagines other scenarios to this frightful scene. He continues the suspense of the story right up to the last moment until Abraham is poised with the dagger over Isaac. Isaac calls out to the Lord to save him. "Good!" says Abraham to himself, "the boy thinks that I want to kill him!" And he drops the knife. The other scenario is equally gripping. Again the suspenseful events are recalled. At the last moment, Abraham drops the knife; he can not go through with this. The result: Isaac never spoke to him from that day forward! What scenario would you choose?

The Old Testament is full of other references to testing, such as the testing of Israel in the desert, but also the testing of the individual (Ps 26:1; 139:23; Prov 3:11–12; Sir 1:2; 4:17–19). So the idea of a test was neither unusual nor even in some cases unwelcome. But there is also the measure of the trial. No one is depicted as being under the strain of Abraham or Job; they were the exemplars: tested, and proved faithful.

A Postil

This title is preferable to postface, which is a recognized correspondent to a preface, with which this book began. "Postil" derives from a medieval phrase, *post illa (verba),* "after those (words)," which designated a series of comments on a biblical work. Dear reader, you have once again, perhaps, read and studied the book of Job, duly aided or even disturbed and distracted by this "short reading." It would be well to return to the question with which we began: "What does it do to you if you read it" Each reader has to give his or her own answer, and there will probably be many variations. The elimination of certain awkward and even misleading detours has been pointed out in the above short reading, and hopefully this will be of some use. It is fitting if I briefly share with you what it does to me.

The fundamental question is: Why does an innocent person suffer? This "why?" is uttered by Job several times, even from the beginning (Job 3:11, 12, 16, 20). But it is never given a positive, rational, answer. This means that I can no longer treat the book of Job as a theodicy, a view held by many, in any shape or form. The attempt to defend the "justice" of a mysterious God is bound to go down in defeat. The friends of Job presented a defense of God in the terms of the biblical understanding at the time, and it is clearly bankrupt. Neither are the other "hints," such as the intervention of Elihu, or even of the Lord, an adequate solution to Job's "why?" They are suggestive, I think, when I have my back up against the wall. But the wall of divine mystery remains standing, impenetrable. I am more on the side of chapter 28: "Where is wisdom to be found?"

Can I live with this? I have to, or else give up hope. A Christian might claim that the solution is to be found in the New Testament, in the death and resurrection of Jesus Christ. That faith is consoling, but it is not an "answer" to Job's question, even if it is perceived to be such. Jesus, too, ran into the impenetrable wall of divine mystery: "Not my will, but yours be done" (Luke 22:42).

Is my predicament all that desperate? Ultimately, yes. But the book of Job does something to me if I read it. It does give an unmistakable new orientation to my desperation. I am no longer the prisoner, of my guilt nor even of my anger, my rage, my grief, my despair, the total outburst of pain. Job has shown me the way, and I can never forget the words of the Lord that Job spoke rightly (42:7). I am challenged to explore how my sufferings, small or great, play out against the background of other possible and perhaps even appropriate reactions. Where do I stand when I suffer? I hold to my understanding and interpretation of 13:15, "Slay me though he might, I will wait for him" (NAB). This is a "tough love" that God shows, but the book of Job suggests that there is no alternative for me.

What works for me may not work for others. Undoubtedly. But that is not the issue. What does the reading of the book of Job do to anyone? Can it not serve as a guide to one who is terminally ill, or simply overwhelmed by life or its absence, such as the starving in the Sudan or the suffering of other desperate people in the world (you name it)? By this I mean that one dare not underrate the power of the word of God if or when it is read by such a person. One must leave open the action of the grace of God upon the suffering who might be engaged with the reading of Job. If by our own wits we attempt to seek consolation or to offer it to others, there is the frightening example of the friends who failed in their effort to deal with Job. They might have been more successful had they continued with the voice of grief and the awesome silence with which they began, 2:12–13. It is a salutary lesson for anyone, however well-meaning, who would offer comfort or sympathy. But then, ironically, we would never have the book of Job.

It is important for me to relate Job to the Psalms and Jeremiah. Job's voice or his fate is not alone in the Old Testament. When I read the laments and complaints in the psalter, there is another "Job" experience: "Have pity on me, Lord, for I am languishing; heal me, Lord, for my body is in terror. My soul, too is utterly terrified; but you, Lord, how long...?" (Ps 6:3–4). The writer of Ps 73 compared his lot with that of the wicked, and envied them: "I almost lost my balance; my feet all but slipped" (73:2). But the psalmist persevered: "To be near God is my good" (73:28). Or I think of Jeremiah, a prophet who put his life on the line for God, and who received such encouraging and consoling promises as, "They will fight against you, but not prevail over you" (Jer 1:19). When he complained bitterly and with reason about those who threatened his life and asked for vengeance, he received the uncomforting reply, "If running against men has wearied you, how will you race against horses…." (Jer 12:5).

Although I have read, preached, lectured and written about the book of Job for many years, I still have reason to wince. Do I really know what I am talking about? Does one have to be a "Job" to speak "correctly?" (42:7). What troubles me is a cartoon that I discovered by sheer luck in a daily newspaper back in 1972. I carry a photocopy of it in my wallet. It is a Goldberg drawing, entitled "Pepper…and Salt." It presents two characters, one with his brushes and paint cans, the other a companion who is apparently voicing an opinion about the drawing of a figure on the standing easel. It is a rather undistinguished sketch that has a distant resemblance to the two characters. The legend beneath them runs, "I'm afraid, Roland, you haven't suffered enough."

Select Bibliography

Alonso Schökel, L., *Job, commentario teologico y literario* (NBE; Madrid: Cristiandad, 1983).

Andersen, F. I., *Job* (Downers Grove, Ill.: InterVarsity Press, 1976).

Clines, D. J., *Job 1–20* (WBC 17; Dallas: Word, 1989).

Green, B., "Recasting a Classic: A Reconsideration of Meaning in the Book of Job," *New Blackfriars* 74/870; April 1993, 213–22.

Greenberg, M. "Job," *The Literary Guide to the Bible* (ed. R. Alter et al., Cambridge: Harvard, 1987), 283–303.

Habel, N. C., *The Book of Job* (OTL; Philadelphia: Westminster, 1985).

Janzen, J. G., *Job* (Interpretation; Atlanta: John Knox, 1985).

Newsom, C. A., "The Book of Job" in *The New Interpreter's Bible* (Nashville: Abingdon, 1996), vol. 4, 319–637.

_____, "Cultural Politics and the Reading of Job," *Biblical Interpretation* 1/2 (1993), 119–38.

Perdue, L. G., and W. C. Gilpin, eds. *The Voice from the Whirlwind: Interpreting the Book of Job* (Nashville: Abingdon, 1992).

Schreiner, S. E., *Where Shall Wisdom Be Found?* (University of Chicago Press, 1994).

Tsevat, M., "The Meaning of the Book of Job," *Hebrew Union College Annual* 37 (1966), 73–106.

Vogels, W., *Job. L'homme qui a bien parlé de Dieu* (Paris: du Cerf, 1995).

Wilcox, J. T., *The Bitterness of Job: A Philosophical Reading* (Ann Arbor: University of Michigan Press, 1989/1984).

Whybray, R. N., *Job* (Sheffield: Sheffield Academic Press, 1998).

Index